UNIVERSITIES AT WAR

SAGE SWIFTS

In 1976 SAGE published a series of short 'university papers', which led to the publication of the QASS series (or the 'little green books' as they became known to researchers). Almost 40 years since the release of the first 'little green book', SAGE is delighted to offer a new series of swift, short and topical pieces in the ever-growing digital environment.

SAGE *Swifts* offer authors a new channel for academic research with the freedom to deliver work outside the conventional length of journal articles. The series aims to give authors speedy access to academic audiences through digital first publication, space to explore ideas thoroughly, yet at a length which can be readily digested, and the quality stamp and reassurance of peer-review.

UNIVERSITIES AT WAR

THOMAS DOCHERTY

Los Angeles | London | New Delhi
Singapore | Washington DC

Los Angeles | London | New Delhi
Singapore | Washington DC

SAGE Publications Ltd
1 Oliver's Yard
55 City Road
London EC1Y 1SP

SAGE Publications Inc.
2455 Teller Road
Thousand Oaks, California 91320

SAGE Publications India Pvt Ltd
B 1/I 1 Mohan Cooperative Industrial Area
Mathura Road
New Delhi 110 044

SAGE Publications Asia-Pacific Pte Ltd
3 Church Street
#10-04 Samsung Hub
Singapore 049483

© Thomas Docherty 2015

First published 2015

Apart from any fair dealing for the purposes of research or private study, or criticism or review, as permitted under the Copyright, Designs and Patents Act, 1988, this publication may be reproduced, stored or transmitted in any form, or by any means, only with the prior permission in writing of the publishers, or in the case of reprographic reproduction, in accordance with the terms of licences issued by the Copyright Licensing Agency. Enquiries concerning reproduction outside those terms should be sent to the publishers.

Editor: Chris Rojek
Assistant editor: Gemma Shields
Production editor: Vanessa Harwood
Marketing manager: Michael Ainsley
Cover design: Jen Crisp
Typeset by: C&M Digitals (P) Ltd, Chennai, India
Printed and bound by CPI Group (UK) Ltd, Croydon, CR0 4YY (for Anthony Rowe)

Library of Congress Control Number: 2014948956

British Library Cataloguing in Publication data

A catalogue record for this book is available from the British Library

ISBN 978-1-4739-0778-2
eISBN 978-1-4739-1062-1

At SAGE we take sustainability seriously. Most of our products are printed in the UK using FSC papers and boards. When we print overseas we ensure sustainable papers are used as measured by the Egmont grading system. We undertake an annual audit to monitor our sustainability.

Thomas Docherty not only is a brilliant critic of those forces that would like to transform higher education into an extension of the market-place and a recruiting tool for the conformist prone, low-paid workforce needed by corporate powers, he is also a man of great moral and civic courage, who under intense pressure from the punishing neoliberal state has risked a great deal to remind us that higher education is a civic institution crucial to creating the formative cultures necessary for a democracy to survive, if not flourish.

Universities at War is both insightful and accessible, and one of the most important books published that deals with the ongoing attacks being waged worldwide on higher education. Docherty defines the university as a worldly institution that cannot be separated from the economic, social, cultural, and political forces in which it is shaped and acts. Few writers make the case for the civic purpose of higher education, for its centrality to democracy, and for its responsibility to educate young people and others to be engaged, critical citizens of the world. This book is a tour de force.
Professor Henry Giroux, McMaster University, Canada

Few people in the UK are able and willing to trace the current university crisis to its cultural, political and economic roots and to challenge the reigning policy orthodoxy in print. None has experienced the war against the universities with anything like the ferocity visited upon Thomas Docherty in 2014. The unique witness of this urgent book demands close attention.
Professor Howard Hotson, St Anne's College, Oxford University

This is the polemos of Thomas Docherty, both polemic and war. It is a polemic about the struggle for the university and the right to higher education. It does not just report that war but participates fully in the ongoing debate, taking a position against the market and in the name of the academy. Docherty is one of our finest literary critics whose writing on the university illuminates its corridors. This is another important intervention by a true resistant for critical thought and the university.
Professor Martin McQuillan, Kingston University

With Stefan Collini, Thomas Docherty is a major contemporary heir to Newman, a defender of a sober, principled, honourable, sophisticated, demanding and by no means idealized concept of the university; this when, in the UK, actual universities sometimes seem increasingly populated by aliens from outer space. The serious intellectual life is in danger of being ruthlessly marginalized,

left to a new breed of peripatetic. If this is not to happen, powerful, ferocious, clever, learned books like *Universities at War* are much-needed.
Andrew Gibson, Former Professor of Modern Literature and Theory, Royal Holloway College, University of London

Thomas Docherty's *Universities at War* is a powerful, erudite polemical study of everything that fails to work so drastically in the institution of higher education. Resisting any temptation to proceed with business as usual, Docherty explores and exposes, with wit, insight, and not a little panache, the Realpolitik of the university-as-business. To ignore this book is to be culpable of the crimes against education, in the name of 'education', which Docherty indicts.
Professor Julian Wolfreys, University of Portsmouth

Docherty engages with the secular university in its present crisis, reflecting on its origins and on its role in the future of democracy. He tackles the urgent issue of inequality with a compelling denunciation of the ways of entrenched privilege; he offers a view of governance and representation from the perspective of those who are silenced; and exposes the fundamental damage done to thought by management-speak. Docherty is moral, passionate and committed this is a fierce and important book.
Professor Mary Margaret McCabe, King's College London

CONTENTS

About the Author   viii
Preface and Acknowledgements   ix

Introduction   1

1 Force or the body politic and the 'sovereignty of nature'   20

2 Debts and Duties or of time and trust in the University   46

3 Citizens, Denizens and Cosmopolitans   75

4 Of Governance and Government   107

Index   143

ABOUT THE AUTHOR

Thomas Docherty is Professor of English and of Comparative Literature in the University of Warwick. He previously held the Chair of English (1867) in Trinity College Dublin, and a Chair Professorship in the University of Kent. He has held many international visiting positions, and has lectured worldwide. He is the author of numerous books, including, most recently, *For the University* (Bloomsbury, 2011), *Confessions: The Philosophy of Transparency* (Bloomsbury, 2012), *The English Question* (Sussex Academic, 2010), *Aesthetic Democracy* (Stanford, 2008). He is currently working on a book about memory, and is also writing an account of some recent events, provisionally called *In Parenthesis: A Year in Suspense.*

PREFACE AND ACKNOWLEDGEMENTS

The university sector worldwide is in turmoil. All governments stress the crucial importance of the institution, and, as a result, they interfere with its workings. Paradoxically, the more that politics insists on the importance of the university globally, the more it actually drives the institution away from material realities and from democratic civil engagement. The greatest interference relates to the monetization of all academic work, such that the university institution becomes eviscerated of all content, including intellectual content. Instead, economic factors determine the identity and even the function of our institutions. Money has systematically replaced thought as the key driver and *raison d'être* of the institution's official existence. That priority has consequences, and among the most serious of these is the determination to *manage* knowledge and its people (students, academics and cultures). Management and control of knowledge has become more important than research, teaching or even thinking and living the 'good life' together.

The consequence of this is a peculiar *stasis*: in ancient Greek, the word meant 'civil war' (though, today, it's the sign at a bus stop). This is paradoxical because the university is subjected to continuous 'change-management'. Within the institutions, everything changes, everyday, according to a myth of 'continuous improvement' and 'dynamic management' in our allegedly 'fast-changing global environment'. Oddly, however, everything stays the same within the societies to whose existence the institution is deemed so socially and politically central. Inequality and injustice persist, and ignorance retains all the seductive force of myth.

This book is written in an effort to find out how the university sits between worldliness on one hand and civic relations on the other hand. It follows on from my earlier study, *For the University*; but while that book focused almost entirely on the United Kingdom, the present one addresses the 'global' institution and has a greater scope and ambit. It is an attempt to formulate arguments that will help us discover the proper forms and functions of a university in our contemporary material or worldly predicaments. The stakes for the future of the institution are extremely high: if the university has a future at all, it has to find its place – even to fight for its place – in the logic of a warring world where civilization itself is endangered.

The final research and writing of this book were carried out under awkward circumstances – while I was suspended from my position at the University of Warwick. During the period of suspension (almost a full year as I write, today, 23 July 2014), I have been supported by family, colleagues and friends. When I was initially suspended, I was told that I was to have no contact with colleagues or students and that, if I did, then such contact would be regarded as actionable under disciplinary procedures that could lead to my summary dismissal from employment. I was also barred from access to campus, and, as a result, some of the documentation for this book has had to be taken from web-sources rather than print-sources, as I could not access the library.

Notwithstanding all this, colleagues and students made contact with me, and, eventually, I was able to communicate at least formally, largely through the efforts of my UCU representative, Dennis Leech. I owe Dennis the gift of that communication, which allowed me to break the enforced isolation imposed on me as a condition of suspension. I want to extend special thanks also to some who maintained close friendly contact, sustaining me throughout: M.M. McCabe, Martin McQuillan, Dan Katz, Carol Rutter and Neil Lazarus. I have had excellent legal and medical support from Ian Besant, Emma-Christine O'Keefe, Katie Lancaster, Paul Greatorex, Katie Lennon, Agi Brenk and Martin Read-Jones. At SAGE, Ziyad Marar, Chris Rojek and Gemma Shields encouraged me in the writing of this book. My debts to all these are incalculable.

I also owe thanks to the many who have found out about my situation, and who have contacted me with messages of support, including Jon Baldwin, Stefan Baumgarten, Eleanor Bell, Jim Byatt, Gordon Campbell, Carlo Caruso, Elizabeth Clarke, Stefan Collini, Nicholas Collins, Nessa Cronin, Valentine Cunningham, Ed Davies, Oliver Davis, Sharae Deckard, Andy Dobson, Dominic Dean, Ana de Medeiros, Paulo de Medeiros, George Donaldson, Robert Eaglestone, Rod Edmond, Alireza Fakhrkonandeh, John Flower, Ross Forman, Larissa Fradkin, Michael Gardiner, Mike Geppert, Andrew Gibson, Lucy Gill, John Gilmore, Priya Gopal, Sorcha Gunne, Paul Hamilton, Simon Head, David Herd, John Holmwood, Howard Hotson, Tony Howard, Michael Hulse, Lyn Innes, Wendy Jacobson, Mary Kelly, Gyorgy Koentges, Nick Lawrence, Caitriona Leahy, Alice Leonard, Graeme Macdonald, Stuart Macdonald, Wallace McDowell, Emma Mason, Jon Mee, David Melville, Drew Milne, Sian Mitchell, Gerald Moore, Philip Moriarty, Emilie Morin, Liz Morrish, Pablo Mukherjee, Stuart Murray, Catalina Neculai, Kerstin Oloff, Tamson Pietsch, Julian Preece, Steve Purcell,

Pierre Purseigle, Adam Putz, Nicholas Roe, Amy Rogers, Ana-Maria Sanchez-Arce, Nima Seifi, Stephen Shapiro, John Sheil, Christian Smith, Roger Sugden, Nima Taleghani, Catherine Toal, Jeremy Treglown, Margaret Tudeau-Clayton, Rashmi Varma, Julian Warner, Steve Waters, Carol Watts, Andy Webb, Claire Westall, Noel Whiteside, Caroline Wintersgill, Rhian Williams, David Wilson. The *Poppletonian*, newspaper of the University of Poppleton, has also featured my predicament; so I should thank its chief reporter, Keith Ponting (30), and Poppleton's key operative, Jamie Targett.

Many others, I gather, have been less confident of contacting me, fearing that they may jeopardize either my own position or theirs if they do so. You know who you are; you know how much your support, even if unexpressed, has sustained me. I hope this book is some repayment.

For my students

INTRODUCTION

> ... And so I was keen to distinguish crooked from straight,
> And to search for truth in the groves of Academe.
> But turbulent times snatched me from that sweet spot ...
>
> (Horace, *Epistles*, 2; 2; ll. 44–46)[1]

1 TURBULENT TIMES

There is a war on for the future of the university as an institution. We find ourselves, like Horace in my epigraph, in 'turbulent times', and, in many jurisdictions across the world, scholars and students are striving to find ways of responding adequately and appropriately to the disturbances that are afflicting societies in both the advanced and the developing economies. In this, of course, they are not unlike other citizens who face the same social, political and economic predicaments. However, they do have one very particular and specific characteristic that marks out the university as a site of special interest.

The current turbulence – post-2008, post-9/11 and post-Arab Spring – can be seen fundamentally as a very precise ideological contest, in which what has been conventionally called the 'life of the mind' struggles with the material realities of 'life on the street' or, more specifically, on the city squares that have witnessed so many protests in recent times. On the one hand, there is the potential presiding power of ideas and ideals (the proper province of the university, one might perhaps think, at least provisionally) to shape the material conditions in which humans will live together; on the other hand, there is the brute material force of history itself and of *Realpolitik*, which takes precedence over any ideals, and which requires that ideals (and universities where such ideals are explored) adjust themselves pragmatically to realities.

---

[1] Trans. A.S. Kline (2005): http://www.poetryintranslation.com/PITBR/Latin/HoraceEpistlesBkIIEpII.htm. See also Horace, *Satires, Epistles and Ars Poetics*, ed. and trans. H. Rushton Fairclough (Loeb Classical Library; Heinemann, 1926), 426–427 for bilingual text.

At one abstract philosophical level, this is the conflict between Hegel and Marx; but I want to explore it in more immediate and concrete terms. It is a contest between 'what is' and 'what ought to be', between practice and theory. That is much more than a simple philosophical debate. In fact, behind it lies a much more profound confrontation of the relative priorities that we will give to history over consciousness or vice versa: does the way we think about the world determine how we shape it, such that our ideas configure historical realities, or do the world's historical forces configure our consciousness, such that we 'reflect' that world and internalize its actualities as a norm of thought? It asks the fundamental question, therefore, concerning the relation of the university as a privileged site of thought to the world in which it finds itself; and it therefore places the student at the central axis of our contemporary turbulence.

In the face of this, in some cases, we have seen students joining with the general aims of the Occupy movement, temporarily occupying university buildings or spaces and 'reclaiming' those spaces in order to return them to their proper use, as a site for debate, criticism and dissent. On this view, the university and the ideas that emanate from dissenting debate can help shape history. Others, by contrast, have sought more immediate and direct action, prioritizing material realities in an effort to change or reconfigure the ideas and ideals around which a society – and its universities, its 'life of the mind' – might organize itself. These latter have started coming out of the libraries and laboratories and on to the streets to join with concerned citizens where, sometimes, they find their right to walk in protest through the streets impeded, and find the full material force of the state, as they are 'kettled' by police forces or are met with other forms of violence. We have seen this struggle for priorities enacted in numerous different jurisdictions. Chile, Québec, Spain and the United Kingdom are the places where the protests and the associated movements have perhaps been most visible; but the International Student Movement details such actions worldwide.[2]

What is it that has so disturbed the *Groves of Academe* about which Mary McCarthy wrote in her campus novel of that title in the United States in 1951? Why might students and scholars feel 'embattled'? What is the nature of the war or struggles at issue, and if there is indeed a war, what is at stake in it? To borrow from the subtitle of *The Rights of Man* by H.G. Wells in 1940, just after the breakout of the Second World War, 'what are we fighting for?' When McCarthy borrowed her novel's title from Horace's *Epistles*, there was a prevalent view of the University as an institution where, indeed, one would set about trying to 'search for truths in the groves of academe', and one would do this by a quiet

---

[2] See, for instance, http://www.emancipating-education-for-all.org.

and meditative attempt to 'distinguish crooked from straight'. The presiding image of the institution, across the developed world of the early 1950s or post-Second World War years, was one where the academy was like a sequestered area in which one could pursue, in a bucolic and undisturbed fashion, the 'life of the mind', untroubled and untrammelled by the cares of the world, fulfilling at last the 19th-century Arnoldian promise that we should find the 'best that has been thought and said' in a supposedly entirely 'disinterested' manner.

This presiding image, of course, was always a myth, and indeed, one of the reasons why the 'campus novel' started to appear as a separate genre in this period, relates precisely to the fact that the institutions, post-Second World War, started to undergo changes to debunk that myth. Such changes, themselves, to some extent, were actually conditioned by war and its socio-cultural aftermath, when the violence of history had disturbed any myth of a culture at peace and intellectual ease with itself. This is perhaps most clear, for a specific example, in the passing of the US GI Bill, or 'Servicemen's Readjustment Act', passed in 1944, which helped finance a tertiary education for American veterans returning from the Second World War. Similar provisions for discharged military service personnel were also enacted elsewhere, and the result is a significant change in the constituency of students now attending universities. This new constituency, further, had been as far removed from a bucolic grove as one could imagine, struggling for basic physical survival in the various terrifying theatres of war all across the world. The consequence of this is a tension – within the university institution itself – between the 'life of the mind' detached from worldly care on the one hand and 'survival of the body' threatened by the environment on the other hand.

In the United Kingdom, there had been similar changes previously, in the wake of the Great War of 1914–1918. Those years saw a series of significant changes domestically, especially in relation to the enhanced socio-political visibility – the material realities – of women as they started to gain the franchise. That struggle for state recognition, of course, was not just grounded in intellectual argument: the suffragettes had recourse to direct and violent action; by the end of the Great War in 1918, the movement could no longer be resisted. The first woman to be elected to the House of Commons in Westminster was Constance Markiewicz, of Sinn Féin, in December 1918. As a representative of Sinn Féin, however, she refused to take her seat in the Westminster government, for she was engaged in a further violent political struggle – a war, in fact – for Irish independence. Consequently, she took her seat instead – alongside some 73 other elected Sinn Féin candidates – as a representative in the newly formed *Dáil Éireann*, claiming independent self-government for the Republic of Ireland. Struggles in war and over gender coalesce in terms of the social and political franchise: women have the right to speak, to vote and to establish their cultural and political authority; but this arises here precisely in the context of warfare.

Hitherto, such authority had been the province of men only, and especially in relation to the UK government, it had been the province of men who not only inherited land, wealth and forms of cultural or official 'entitlement', but also became members of an 'establishment' through their university degrees and the networks that they had established in Oxbridge. War was putting this kind of unquestioned entitlement under severe pressure and scrutiny (though the establishment fought back vigorously). In 1919, for example, the United Kingdom's 'Sex Disqualification Removal Act' opened numerous professions to women for the first time. War – together with a female workforce that had found their social voice more audibly when men were away at the front – had shifted society from its usual bearings and previous norms. Further, soon after this, women were allowed not only to attend university but also to proceed to take their degrees formally. This also significantly changed the university, bringing new constituencies into daily contact with each other, and doing so under the aegis of political struggles and international war.

Class also started to play a major role in this series of social changes occasioned by war, and one place where class would make its presence felt most directly was education. In 1918, Herbert Fisher, the Liberal President of the Board of Education in David Lloyd George's wartime government, proposed a new Education Act. The Education Act of 1918 not only raised the school-leaving age to 14, but also envisaged a growth in the tertiary sector. Paragraph 3:2 of Chapter 39 is explicit in requiring the 'cooperation of universities' in providing a higher education for any student for whom it would be appropriate. In this, the Fisher Act of 1918 is a clear forerunner and harbinger of the better-known Robbins Report of 1963, which asserted that university places should be available to all and to those who had shown that they could benefit from it or who were qualified 'by ability and attainment'.

Fisher's Act was followed in 1919 with the formal establishment of the University Grants Committee. This Committee did two very significant new things. First, it helped to establish, for the first time, a self-consciously national state-funded university system in the United Kingdom. The state demonstrated a fundamental financial commitment and declared an interest, an interest on behalf of the general population as a national whole. Second, it helped secure more sustainable state funding for the existing institutions (Oxbridge, London, some late 19th-century institutions) that had been damaged or substantially under-funded as a result of the war effort.

During the war years, research funding provided to the universities had not only been significantly reduced but had also been instrumentalized and concentrated directly on problems and issues associated with the war itself. In 1918, Lord Richard Haldane (who, in earlier years, had been Secretary of State for War) produced his celebrated report, written explicitly in an address to the aftermath of this situation. The Haldane Report argued for a judicious separation between the interests of the state (or the political determination of research priorities) on one hand and the interests of scholarly pursuit of research and truth (the clichéd 'first casualty of war'), or that Horatian distinction of the 'crooked from the straight', on the other hand. The result is a general principle designed to protect the university from direct governmental control and inappropriate interference, while still allowing for the state to exert an influence commensurate with and warranted by its commitment of a substantial financial interest.

The Haldane principle is there to ensure that the university has protection against the political manipulation of societal norms, especially norms concerning the true or the good: in short, it protects the university from becoming a machine for the enhancement or validation of political propaganda and dogma. This principle – although often subverted – persists, at least in theory, to the present times. In Germany, in 1946, it found equivalent expression as 'academic freedom' in Jaspers' *Idea of the University*, a text re-written to protect the German sector from any possibility of a repeat of Nazi politicization. The important issue here, though, is that it is a fundamental principle governing the modern university that derives specifically and directly from war and its aftermath[3].

'Turbulent times' might properly be seen precisely as a kind of basic condition governing the shape of the modern university. This gives a specific inflection to my opening claim that there is a war on for the future of the university itself: in one sense, the very constitution of the university as an institution is intimately related to – even conditioned by – war itself. However, one aspect of the contemporary war is that it is a war that is being waged *against* the university, paradoxically, at a time when nation states across the world are vaunting their universities flamboyantly. The contemporary war of which I write in this book, as I will show, is partly for the very survival of the university in the 21st century.

2 THE ELITIST MYTH AND LIFE ON THE STREET

The university is an institution that is not much understood in our times. One of the reasons for this is that it is surrounded by mythology. At one level, this is hardly surprising. Despite the fact that the modern institution is avowedly

---

[3] For Haldane, see http://www.publications.parliament.uk/pa/cm200809/cmselect/cmdius/168/16807.htm. Cf. Karl Jaspers, *The Idea of the University* (1923; revised edition 1946).

given over to mass education, it nonetheless retains its status as something rather distanced from the everyday material life of most of the population. The mythologies of 'ivory towers' or of the privileged world of *Brideshead Revisited* still exert a powerful hold on the cultural imagination.

Historically, the myths that informed the university from its earliest days were those of religion: in its medieval and early modern guise, the university existed to produce or inculcate priesthoods, elite cults whose authority was vested in their priests by otherworldly or supernatural deities and not by worldly powers or by the force of reason. As I will discuss in this book, this persists surprisingly well in the modern condition, even if our 'enlightened' times sit less amicably with supernatural or even religious fundamentalisms.

The institution's status, deriving originally from this elitism associated with religion, is also an issue in its mythologization. The modern university's business often appears to be otherworldly, in that its scientists deal with future and as-yet-unrealized possibilities, while its social scientists and humanities colleagues find plenty of reason to be critical of the everyday world in which they sit. There is an almost necessary disconnection between the world-as-it-is-perceived in its mundane everyday ordinariness on the one hand and the world-as-it-might-be through the interventions of sciences, technologies or imaginations of the extraordinary on the other hand. Distinction such as this leads to the image of elitism, exclusiveness and, worst of all, disengagement from the world. Yet it might be fairer to say that, almost by definition as a research institution, the very character of the university must be one that explicitly distances itself from the here-and-now of material realities, in the search for novelty or innovation. Such distancing, however, need not be 'unworldly'; rather, it might more properly be considered to be just 'critical' of the existing world state of affairs, dissident with respect to it.

Traditionally however, at least in 'the modern tradition', the university retains this character as exclusivist, and as a site of elitist privilege. It even endorses privilege, in some views, not just because it has usually been so long 'occupied' by the privileged classes, but because it is seen as being primarily 'for' those classes, as their preserve or province. That is to say: the institution is inhabited by people divorced from the sphere of everyday struggles, even if they are enmeshed in allegedly 'higher-level' struggles, with some mysterious and enigmatic entity called 'knowledge', the discovery of the 'straight' as opposed to the 'crooked' in the life of the mind as opposed to the life on the streets.

How relevant is this 'life on the street'? London taxi drivers – their lives lived on the streets, literally – also have 'The Knowledge'. To ply their trade as taxi drivers, they need to pass an examination – colloquially referred to as 'The

Knowledge' – demonstrating that they can take a passenger between any two designated points in London by the shortest route: straight, not crooked, as in Horace. This requires a detailed knowledge of some 50,000 places of interest, around 24,000 streets and roads and innumerable intersections that can allow for an alarming number of permutations. The Knowledge therefore requires geographical thinking, mathematical computation, often linguistic competence, anthropological understanding and understanding of the city as a social and political terrain, not to mention a compendious memory. It takes a good student at least three years of study to get The Knowledge to a degree where she or he can pass the test; but the average length of study is in fact closer to five years. It is also a life-long learning, as the city and its layout change on a daily basis.

In one way, this all sounds a bit like a very-high-level university degree, with a massive interdisciplinary range. Yet the status of the university degree and its specific type of knowledge is different, and it is so precisely because it is often thought of as having little or nothing to do with the life on the streets, with the city or polity and with the commerce of everyday material practices of just getting from here to there. The taxi driver's knowledge is 'of the world' in ways that a degree is not: it is 'mundane', where the university's knowledge is mythic or literally 'extraordinary', out of and beyond the ordinary, the quotidian or mundane. This different status is important, and it gives a specific set of problems to the university as a modern institution.

The real and fundamental question that I am addressing here relates to what we might call the *secular* university. In earlier periods, the priorities of the university were essentially non-secular, and it was through its claims to have access to the non-secular – its theocentric or cultic ground – that gave it its massive cultural authority. This prioritization of the non-secular remained in place even when worldly and material realities – especially conflicts that are related to wars – intervened directly in the operations of the institutions.

At the turn of the 15th century in Europe, we saw the beginning of an expansion of the university institution across the continent. The reasons for this were at once secular *and* theological. In 1417, a great controversy – the Great Schism – in the Catholic Church in Europe was resolved, at least temporarily; but the Schism itself, and its resolution, had consequences for the university as an institution. Prior to the ending of the Avignon papacy, it was fairly commonplace for scholars to travel to what was, at the time, a relatively small number of European institutions. Scholars from Scotland and England, for instance, would attend institutions in Bologna, Salerno, Paris, Orléans and so on. The emergence of two popes, however, contesting the papacy itself, had consequences especially for those scholars from Scotland.

When England sided with Rome, the Scots backed Avignon. This made travel – to Bologna or Salerno or Paris, say – somewhat difficult for the Scottish scholars, given that they had to traverse the foreign terrain of a different theocracy in England. Given this new political situation, what happened, in Scotland in this instance, was the inauguration and development of new institutions, such as St Andrews University. This, like Glasgow or Aberdeen, is an institution that was established in the face of directly historical political events, involving potential conflict between nation states. Yet, the institution itself remains firmly grounded in unearthly matters, in faculties such as theology, and the university remains an institution for the maintenance of what are profoundly non-secular concerns.

Indeed, this is, for many centuries, the typical European model of the foundation of the university as a site of 'higher' education. The issue has to do with what we mean by 'higher' itself. The very word connotes hierarchy, but it also suggests that there is a fundamental gap between what we think of as the ordinary – the mundane – and a mind that is focused on worlds deemed to be 'higher' than our own. The result of the fundamental persistence of this idea is that the university comes to be seen, even in its modern incarnations, as precisely otherworldly, not of the world, not pertinent to the daily conditions of 'ordinary' or mundane life where we might want a taxi driver to get us from one place to another by the shortest and therefore cheapest route.

3 FICTIONS AGAINST FASCISM

What, then, is a 'secular university', a university that might find a way of regulating the competing demands of life on the street and life in the mind? First and foremost, it might be the institution characterized by its engagement with the world in all its material force and reality. This would be as far removed from the mythic 'ivory tower' as possible. We already have at least one explicitly 'secular' institution, in the form of University College London, founded in 1826 as an institution whose students would not need to swear a religious affiliation. However, by the 'secular university', I mean something different from this and more far-reaching: the secular institution is one that is concerned above all with worldliness, with the countering of its own myth.

In 1966, Frank Kermode made a useful observation on myth in his study *The Sense of an Ending*. There, in a book about narrative, Kermode distinguishes between myths and fictions. The key difference is one of attitude, and specifically our attitudes towards history and the ways in which we make sense of our world. We make sense of our present moment in the world by positing hypothetical or provisional endings – fictional endings, as it were – for our present actions. The ending – how we think things will pan out – allows us to make sense of the present reality. Following logically, Kermode then argues that 'Fictions are for finding things out, and they change as the needs of sense-making change'. In contrast, 'Myth operates within the diagrams of ritual, which presupposes total and adequate explanations of things as they are and were; it is a sequence of radically unchangeable gestures'.

In the present context, this helps us distinguish between a university that is grounded in myths of 'total and adequate explanations of things as they are' on the one hand and a university that is 'for finding things out' and thereby required to 'change as the needs of sense-making change' on the other hand. The extraordinary significance of this is clarified by Kermode's choice of examples to help us not just distinguish myth from fiction, but also to see how high the stakes are in making the distinction correctly. 'Fictions', he writes, 'can degenerate into myths whenever they are not consciously held to be fictive. In this sense anti-Semitism is a degenerate fiction, a myth; and *Lear* is a fiction'. Summing up, he writes that 'Myths call for absolute, fictions for conditional assent'.[4]

We can see here how politically important it is to reconsider the mythic version of the university, and to ask the institution to reconsider its own self-understanding. The persistence of myth – with its fundamentalist claims for absolute assent, for immutable and implacable authority – endangers not just the institution, but also the people among whom such a dangerous fundamentalism arrogantly parades itself. Authoritarian terror – for that is what it is, in the end – has to be challenged by the opening of fictions, for purely conditional and provisional assent to the existing ways of the world. It is only thus that the university can entertain change at all; and therefore it is also only thus that the university can be genuinely historical, subject to change: secular, critical of 'how it is'.

This book, then, is not some appeal to a mythic golden age, nor is it an appeal for a university that claims any foundational or fundamentalist claims for the organization of ritualized and unchanging societies or worlds. Rather, I begin from the premise that the university, like fiction, helps us to make changes and to inhabit a world of constant change. In short, there is an intimate and necessary relation between the university and history itself and between the university and secularity.

In recent times, the 'higher' of higher education in the university has also come to relate precisely to a profound worldly issue: the issue of class and of privilege. This can be discerned precisely by looking at some relevant fictions.

The period between, say, *Brideshead Revisited* in 1945 and *Lucky Jim* in 1957 would be instructive here. Waugh's novel, written towards the end of the war

---

[4] Kermode, *The Sense of an Ending* (Oxford University Press, 1966), 39.

and largely conditioned by it, is explicitly a fiction concerned with the construction of Oxford University and of student life there as a site that is entirely opposite to the experience of war. The privations of war are replaced with high aestheticism in relation to art, botany, the language of flowers, politics, plentiful food and drink. At the core of this is the construction of Oxford as somehow axiomatically the site of nostalgia or of idealized memory or fantasy, including infantile fantasies associated with the teddy bear, Aloysius.

Waugh himself was clear that the text was a product of its time, in the sense that it tried more or less explicitly to run away from its time. In the preface to the revised edition that he wrote in 1959, he pointed out that the book was written with zest: 'It was a bleak period of present privation and threatening disaster – the period of soya beans and Basic English – and in consequence the book is infused with a kind of gluttony, for food and wine, for the splendours of the recent past, and for rhetorical and ornamental language, which now with a full stomach I find distasteful'.[5] Although he describes his own condition as one of impatience to get back to war, the novel itself celebrates this avoidance of what we might call 'mundane life'.

One interesting thing relates to the dates here. Waugh published *Brideshead Revisited* in 1945, the year after the UK Government passed the 1944 Education Act, the 'Butler Act' (passed on 3 August 1944). This Act was designed, among other things, to deal with the legacy of the Second World War, for whose end and aftermath the government of the day was already preparing. Specifically, the United Kingdom knew that its basic class infrastructure had been disturbed by war and that it would have to change. Children, especially those who had been evacuated from less wealthy areas of cities and relocated to homes in the wealthier countryside and shires, now knew a world that was different from what they had left behind in the more impoverished cities.

The Butler Act helped extend the school-leaving age to 15 (and envisaged 16 as the preferred norm), and it provided access to extended education for many children whose families would not have been able to afford it. In 1938, before the war, around 80% of children left school at age 14, the earliest possible moment. After the Second World War and the Butler Act, that changed significantly. Specifically, the introduction of the '11-plus' exam enabled a patrician Tory view of 'merit', through which Butler and his conservative allies believed they could address the intrinsic inequalities engendered by class, wealth and privilege. Anyone, from any background, who passed this exam was now much more likely to proceed to extended secondary education.

---

[5] Evelyn Waugh, *Brideshead Revisited* (1945; reprinted, Penguin, London, 2000), 7.

This, then, affected children who would have been aged 4 or 5 in 1944. By 1957, then – the year in which Kingsley Amis published *Lucky Jim* – these children would be 18 and would be seeking places in tertiary and university education. This – together with the later changes enabled by the 1963 Robbins Report – might help explain what would become the flowering of a new genre of fiction, the 'campus novel'.

Just before Waugh wrote his 1959 Preface, in which he indicated his slight feelings of shame at the opulence that was celebrated in *Brideshead*, Kingsley Amis wrote what might be seen as one of the first of the United Kingdom's version of that newly emergent strain of campus novels. In 1957, *Lucky Jim* is also infused with issues of class and privilege. Jim Dixon is a lower-middle-class interloper into the 'higher' establishment of much more posh and assuredly self-important academic life; his status as an outcast of sorts, while a long-standing staple of British fiction, is also here related more or less directly to an image of the university and the academy as a body divorced from worldly realities, precisely the realities of living as experienced by the less affluent social orders. (Wartime rationing had only just ceased in the United Kingdom in 1954, for instance.) Dixon has been trying to secure his academic position, and his tenure, by publishing some research. His departmental head, Welch, asked what his article's title is. Jim was dumbfounded: 'it was the prospect of reciting the title of the article he'd written. It was a perfect title, in that it crystallized the article's niggling mindlessness, its funereal parade of yawn-enforcing facts, the pseudo-light it threw upon non-problems'.[6]

Yet, the 'university novel' in the United Kingdom, or *Professorroman* (as Elaine Showalter calls it), predates the specifically Redbrick 'campus'-based novel, *Lucky Jim*, by some half a decade. In 1951, C.P. Snow had published *The Masters*. This novel rather took for granted the sybaritic comforts of an Oxbridge life, for it was concerned with the internal politicking that goes on in the attempt to find a new Master of a Cambridge college. Yet, even in a novel such as this, which at first glance might seem self-satisfied, insular and parochial, the pressures of war and of the outside world are ineradicably there. As Elaine Showalter puts it, in her *Faculty Towers*: 'Cambridge is very much a sanctuary…where the dons are… protected from the rough and tumble outside the walls. But, at the same time, Snow was among the first to show the deadly serious and highly worldly machinations of university politics and their relation to the political machinations outside in an ugly dark decade'.[7]

---

[6] Kingsley Amis, *Lucky Jim* (1954; reprinted, Penguin, Harmondsworth, 1968), 14.

[7] Elaine Showalter, *Faculty Towers* (University of Pennsylvania Press, 2009), 16.

The Masters is set in 1937, and one of the candidates for election to Master, Thomas Crawford, takes a stand against appeasement of Hitler. His worldly politics, however, come into conflict with internal university politics, where it is felt that he lacks the personal touch required of a Master: he might take an admirable political stance, but does he 'fit in'? His rival for the post, Paul Jago, has more of the admired personal skills that engender comfort among his peers; but his wife is something of an embarrassment. The dons face a quandary. Yet, also and more importantly, at the core of this text we find an image of what we might call 'unwarranted authority'. Many, if not most, of the dons who will vote a new Master into place are themselves either burnt-out as scholars or, more often, academics who are not burnt-out because they were never fired up in the first place. They enjoy the privileges of their university life but seem to have done little to earn them. A mere five years or so later, however, with the university institution now well established beyond Oxbridge and with the children of the Butler Act now attending university in greater numbers, the time is propitious for *Lucky Jim*, in which class and the prejudices associated with unearned authority become central social concerns. This is especially the case for a rising middle class who are in university for the primary and express purpose of earning their authority, or 'social and cultural capital', as we would call it after Bourdieu.

Interestingly, across all these texts, the material realities of existence that are being avoided — or dealt with by extreme circumlocution — also appear to be linked at various stages to sexual activity. One possible reason for this is hypothesized by Showalter when she writes — perhaps with Plato's *Symposium* somewhere in mind — that 'few professors can survive an academic career without acknowledging the erotic tensions of teaching' (p. 120). When gender equality issues come again to the fore socially, this 'erotic tension' will become thematized in the mature campus novels of Lodge and of Bradbury in the United Kingdom or in Alison Lurie or Richard Russo in the United States. The material realities of a war that had shaped Waugh or Snow have now shifted focus, and, as societies moved out from the direct aftermath of the Second World War, they become more or less explicitly refocused in campus fiction on cultural wars or conflicts. The wars in question now, therefore, are wars in which culture itself plays a decisive role: issues of sexual activity, which could be presented as intimate concerns within the closed world of the bedroom, are explicitly related to the social conditioning of gender roles, to sexism that is both institutional and political and to the discontents of the world beyond the bedroom.

Sexuality, however, is just one of the key locations for this interplay, and the interplay in question is always conflictual: a war between the sexes or wars over other issues that the times have felt to be culturally significant. In Lodge's 1975 *Changing Places*, for example, we have a novel structured around a classic opposition between an adventurous, thrusting America and a rather stolidly steady British empiricism. Morris Zapp, the American professor immersed in high-flying 'theory' (allegedly modelled on Stanley Fish), changes places with Philip Swallow, the resolutely 'common-sense' and empirically 'grounded' English academic. In Bradbury's *The History Man*, published at this same time, we find a similar contestation in which the trendily radical would-be revolutionary sociologist, Howard Kirk, claims to be having real-world effects through his teaching. However, the only real effect he seems to have is one of minor and parochial disturbance within the walls of the university or his own study, which serves as a kind of boudoir for sexual shenanigans with colleagues or students. This remains the case until his wife Barbara attempts suicide in the novel's closing paragraph: a real historical matter that occurs while Howard remains self- and sex-obsessed in his basement with Annie Callendar.

A different example of ways in which sexual mores operate as a hinge between the academy and the world is found in some US campus novels. This permeates those novels of Roth (such as *The Professor of Desire*) or Bellow (*The Dean's December; Ravelstein*) that have academics or intellectuals at their core. It also has a resonance elsewhere, as in the South Africa, of Coetzee's *Disgrace*. Yet it is not only sex that 'hinges' worldliness and university. In more recent texts, such as Richard Russo's comic *Straight Man*, it is the economic issue that presses most insistently. Hank Devereaux is heading the English department in Railton, and the key question right the way through the novel is 'which colleagues will be fired to cut costs' for the coming year. Job insecurity and its relation to the precariousness of lives in times of economic crisis – in this case the late 1990s United States – become central preoccupations.

Yet, while this novel was being written, the US economy was booming in general terms. The text bears witness instead to the ways in which that economy is increasingly privatized: through the post-Reagan, post-Thatcher and post-1989 years, previously commonly shared wealth was systematically being transferred into ever-smaller numbers of private hands, and the publicly funded university was being 'unmade', as Christopher Newfield puts it. The so-called 'culture wars' were wars launched by the neo-conservative US right wing, as a means of de-legitimizing the public university. That kind of institution is being replaced by one where the economic norms are insistently being driven towards a logic of privatization, and the result of this is that jobs in the previously secure public sector university are becoming precarious.

The logic is clear: if you want to keep your job, toe wherever you think the line is, and that line is being drawn by 'line managers' who care little for what goes on in the classroom, but who must ensure that whatever goes on there is in no way critical of neo-liberal human resource management. That is to say: *Straight Man*, though comic, nonetheless helps dramatize the ways in which academic freedom – the freedom to criticize or dissent – is threatened, and the key to the threat is a simulated 'war' in which the neo-conservative Right alleges that dissident thinking – Kermode's provisional fiction-making, open-ended entertainment of change – endangers the 'unchanging gestures' of 'total and adequate explanation' of things as they are, and things therefore as they need to remain.

As in the United States and its 'unmaking' of the public university, so also in the United Kingdom, where the 1988 Education Act abolishes tenure and prepares the ground for what becomes a systemic attack on academic freedom in the emergent privatized and corporate UK university. There, one has to discover an allegiance to the university and its commercial 'brand' (which means toeing a corporate line), and not to the demands of one's disciplinary search to distinguish the crooked from the straight. The crooks, instead, have begun their takeover from Russo's 'straight man'. It is not funny.

Through all this, the key thing to note is the sudden prevalence, worldwide, of this new genre of campus novel in the wake of social and political developments after the Second World War and the end of an imperial age. Two reasons for such a literary flowering suggest themselves. First is the opening of many Creative Writing departments, where practicing and established writers can be guaranteed an income from the university in which they teach. Second, however, is the more important reason: over the last fifty years or so, there has been an abiding question for advanced and developing economies worldwide, concerned with establishing the proper relation between the university and the wider economics of societies. This is a question that will determine the extent of state commitment, financially and otherwise, to the university as an institution, and it therefore assumes a central importance in relation to that long-standing question of whether consciousness shapes history or history shapes consciousness.

In all of these texts, the key is that the academic is characterized as one who – despite grounded common sense or the express desire for political engagement – turns away from the world, from the boardroom, and concentrates instead on the book, on the bedroom or on the wage packet. There is no better place, perhaps, for the exercise of myth than this. In short, the textual presentation of the modern and contemporary university yields an image of an out-of-touch and narcissistically self-important clique, concerned to preserve its own status by conservatively asserting the primacy of memory, the rights of privilege and a cult-like access to allegedly eternal unchanging truths. That is to say, the usual presentation of the university is a dominant image of fundamentalism, the fundamentalism of privilege.

It is in the face of this that the secular university, we might say, needs to be brought into existence.

4 'THIS IS THIS'

Myth, today, is 'a type of speech', wrote Barthes. But that was not 'today', that was in 1957. Myth, for Barthes who wrote *Mythologies*, was a language; and, most especially, it was a language that occluded the historical and material vagaries of culture under an allegedly neutral, unchanging and essential nature. That is to say, myths arose whenever things that were culturally constructed were given the appearance of being essentially entirely natural, and myth, therefore, became a specific structure of thinking. It was mythic thinking that arrested criticism, by suggesting, essentially, that reality was some kind of absolute, non-contestable sphere and that our task was simply to live with it. In short, myth says that 'this is this'.

'This is this': the phrase, although ostensibly extremely simple and straightforward, is itself an interesting figure of speech. It can be sententious; it is an example of ellipsis, of brachylogia, even of anaphora or antanaclasis. But in my usage of it here, it is a quotation and one that takes us again to war.

In Michael Cimino's 1978 Vietnam War movie, *The Deer Hunter*, the character of Michael (Robert de Niro), frustrated at how Stanley (John Cazale) is always freeloading, refuses to lend him a pair of boots to go hunting. The scene is one where Michael claims that Stanley is always unprepared, that he always comes deer hunting but without the proper equipment, and he, Mike, has now had enough. He refuses to give Stan his spare boots. 'What's this?' asks Stanley, meaning 'what's going on here; what's the meaning of this?' and, in reply, while holding up a bullet, Michael says, 'See this, Stanley? This is this. This ain't something else. This ... is this. From now on, you're on your own'.

'This is this' at one level signals the call of a reality: things are as they are. It also (via metaphor) signals the end of metaphor and thus the end of the kind of mythology that Barthes had described some two decades earlier. In many ways – and certainly from the point of view of *Mythologies* – it is the most important scene in the entire film. The film is centred on a specific 'frontier' mythology that shapes the idea of the United States, and, when Mike makes his 'This is this' statement, what he is doing is claiming an access to a reality that is beyond representation: it just *is*. However, this fundamental reality of the American psyche as conditioned by the adventurous frontier mythology, as the film will go on to show, is itself equally mythic. In its place, the film will eventually centre precisely on the material reality of that bullet, when Nick (Christopher Walken) shoots himself in the head in the final realization of the film's central motif of America's imperialist war in Vietnam as a gamble that is as mad and self-harming as Russian Roulette.

Here, 'This is this' sets up an opposition between symbol (Michael's bullet) as myth – which stands as incontrovertible, unchanging, essential – and reality (Nick's bullet) as history – which stands characterized by change, possibility and even death. What happens here is that myth – a cultural condition masquerading as nature – is aligned with an unchanging and natural state of affairs. 'This is this', and there is nothing more to say, no possibility of saying – as in every foundational act of criticism – that 'this' may be other than it appears. However, in the movie, it also represents a turning point in the relation between Michael and the others, and especially between Michael and Stan. That turning point is a moment when 'this' can and must become 'that' or when this becomes other-than-this: change, and, in the end a history that leads towards the death of Nick.

This is a model for the contemporary predicament facing the university, in the sense that the university is caught between the preservation of truth (seen, however erroneously, as eternal and unchanging, as the facts of history and of its scientific and cultural artefacts or knowledge) and the inauguration of history (its contribution to making new and future possibilities for human beings and their societies). The institution of the university is caught in a fundamental conflict between the fixity of myth and an agency of change. This dilemma describes the war around secularity that confronts the modern university.

The key function of myth, for a thinker like Mircea Eliade in his *Myth and Reality*, is that it gives us narratives to live by: it provides exemplary paradigms of a general nature that can then be applied to particular instances. It thus operates as a series of normative practices governing 'diet or marriage, work or education, art or wisdom'[8]. In short, it is what gives significance to otherwise merely passing time: it gives meaning to nature, as it were. However, given its narrative and fictional form, it allows for those meanings to change.

Whenever it assumes a position of naturalness and of fundamental stability and intrinsic immutable resistance to change, myth operates a little like ideology. It shapes our norms as individuals and as a society. This was really what Barthes was after, and he therefore proposes the study of mythologies as a study in 'demystification'. In turn, this suggests a certain enigmatic status for myth: it relates to mystery, to knowledge and to initiated knowledge: in short, to the cult.

Following this, I suggest that myth is indeed central to an ideology of education, but to one that is focused on the cult, on cult-value and on a particular

---

[8] Mircea Eliade, *Myth and Reality* (Harper and Row, New York, 1968), 8.

idea of culture, in which 'culture' is construed as a series of unchanging static immutable monuments, like the sacred texts of a canon whose meaning is already finalized, presupposing 'total and adequate explanations of things as they are' as in Kermode. That view translates culture – and with it education – into a commodity form, or something 'radically unchangeable'.

Yet, how is it that myth has anything to do with the university? After all, given the advances of science and of the rational scientific method, how does myth survive in a modernity that is characterized by demystifications of nature through the progressive use of enlightened reason?

This is a question that Hans Blumenberg asks in his *Work on Myth*. He argues that the usual Enlightenment mode suggests that we have moved from *mythos* to *logos*, from myth to reasoned speech and logic. Yet, against this, Romanticism, suspicious of science and its claims for absolute truth, revives myth in various ways. The modern resolution of these, and of the conflict between Enlightenment and Romanticism, is one whereby we retain the power of myth, he says, but we relocate it, removing it from our understanding of real-world history and placing it instead in the purely aesthetic realm. In short, myth is what Ernst Cassirer called 'a symbolic form'. For Blumenberg, though, this is not yet enough.

Blumenberg argues that myth emerges because of the conditions in which 'man' emerges historically. Considered anthropologically, he suggests that when we first stood upright, we found ourselves unfit for the environment: unlike everything else in the world that we were now disrupting by our stance, we had no properly assigned or proper place. In short, we were 'without a clearly defined biological niche'. We thus faced what Blumenberg calls 'the absolutism of reality' – what I have referred to here as the 'This is this' moment. This absolutism of reality, fundamentally, is the realization of the biological fact of the necessity of dying, the fact of historical change itself.

The existing world is indifferent to us, and, as a consequence, we describe that impersonal world order as a kind of 'Fate' or *Ananke*, Necessity. However, our standing upright – our agency – is precisely the event that characterizes us as historical beings, not conditioned by Necessity but engaged with it and at war with it. Faced with this predicament of our biological arbitrariness, we now therefore produce cults and cultures: cultural and symbolic forms that respond, fundamentally, to our bio-political condition.

Myth here is a response to the problem that we can never be free of biological origins. We have myth because we are mortal, and because we live in a specific kind of temporality that entails our death, our demise and the end of things for us. Worse: this end is something that ignores us, for the world continues perfectly well without us. That is to say: myth responds to our existential contingency. The result of this is that we produce culture and education, and one key institution focused on this war between necessity and existential change, between fate and history, is the university.

5 ENLIST IN THE WAR EFFORT

This book tracks the condition of the modern and contemporary university. It explores the relation of the 'life of the mind' and its ability to distinguish the crooked from the straight, with the 'turbulent times' that condition our contemporary world of higher education. Its core argument is that the university is a worldly institution – i.e., that it is and must be secular and that it is fully enmeshed in and of the material and historical world.

The logic of the book's argument derives from this. First, I analyse the relation between the university and the general condition of 'force'. Considered from the point of view of physics (or at least from a very basic view), the material world hangs together as a consequence of the play of forces – *die Spannung* – that yield its very shape or spatial configuration. That play of forces also subtends the less directly physical manifestations of power or authority that constitutes forms of sociopolitical government or micro-level governance of behaviours. A key question here relates to what power or authority a university might have within its society or culture. Alongside force in these general terms, there comes also a consideration of the ways in which violence – not just martial violence as in war, but violence more generally – has played a part in the formation of the modern and contemporary university.

The world, however, is not just an organization of space. It has a temporal secular component as well. This temporal structure is experienced most directly by the contemporary student in terms of the present shaping of her or his future and in terms of a question of debt. The contemporary student is constituted as indebted, primarily through the prevailing tuition fee structures that pave the way for privatization of the sector as a whole. Debt, as deferred payment, involves the student in a profoundly temporal relation to her or his studies. At issue here is the general economic relation of debt to capital itself, and, more specifically, how the university mediates or regulates the relation between student debt and the modes of capital that shape the contemporary historical moment. This involves a widening of the question of debt to include notions of 'duty', and thus also of social taxation as our 'dutiful' commitment to others.

'Duty' to what? This is the core of my chapter on the 'global citizen' that so many institutions now claim that they 'produce'. The university clearly has a deep relation to citizenship in various ways. It operates within the civic polity, and it has some relation to civic life and to civility or civilization. The condition of citizenship presupposes a community that lives in some sense of relation or relatedness, a community based on the fundamentally ethical principles of having due regard for each other. Yet this is under pressure in an increasingly atomized world, where individuals are enjoined to consider their relations with all others as essentially privatized and contractual relations, engaged for the moment of the transactional contract and with no duties beyond that. In short, we are required to be a society not of citizens bound by loyalties but rather of consumers separated by wealth, and our social life is reduced to the activity of shopping. At the same time, however, and despite this tendency to atomized privatization, the very realm of privacy itself is under threat. The chapter here explores the relation of citizenship to global surveillance, especially in an age of capitalist globalization, and it places the university at the epicentre of those relations.

The closing chapter then turns to explore the relations between political government and institutional governance. If the university is indeed an institution in and of the world, then we have a duty to consider how it works internally to see how its mode of governance is consistent with policy and political modes of government. At one surprising point in his writings on *Open Society: Reforming Global Capitalism*, George Soros (2000) addresses the relation between the economy and modes of government. 'Capitalism and democracy', he writes, 'do not necessarily go hand in hand'. Indeed, he goes on to argue that the proper word for a too easy intimacy between government and business is precisely 'fascism'. While we may not want to go this far or to be this specific (though Soros himself may have adequate biographical reason for going this far), we might limit ourselves to observing that a too cosy relation between business and government is typical of systems and polities that are corrupt. The argument of this chapter is that we find both freedom and democracy under threat within our institutions and that this relates to the ways in which freedom and democracy are in straitened circumstances in the wider polity of the advanced and the developing nation states. Authoritarianism, especially within the university, has been embraced as a mode of governance that requires compliance with unearned authority and, in some cases, with governments of dubious legitimacy. Thus, this chapter addresses the tendency to corruption that is becoming not only too apparent but also endemic within our institutional system.

There is a war on for the future of the university, and the students of today and tomorrow need to win it. I write this book in the hope that you will join them.

1
FORCE OR THE BODY POLITIC AND THE 'SOVEREIGNTY OF NATURE'

I obeyed, I suppose, an innate feeling ... which held that hierarchies founded on privilege and money were the worst offence against nature.

(François Mitterrand, Ma Part de Vérité, quoted in Short, Mitterrand, p. 261)

1.1 THE ANATOMY OF CAMPUS VIOLENCE

The university, as an institution that is both in the world and of the world, has a particular relation with force. That relation is not just to be found in its physics laboratories, those spaces on the campus where we explore the forces that constitute the world and worldliness, the way that the world and indeed our universe hangs together by a play of material forces (mass, density, gravitational pull, atomic energy and so on). I mean more than this. The university has a relation to what we can call the politics of force, to the ways in which force shapes the polity. What, then, is the proper relation of the *worldly University* to *civil society* itself?

In the wake of the student revolutions of 1968, Hannah Arendt produced an extended essay, *On Violence*. There, she pondered the relations of violence to power, strength, authority and, crucially, force itself. She ponders carefully the precise meanings of these terms and indicates that '*Force*, which we often use in daily speech as a synonym for violence, especially if violence serves as a means of coercion, should be reserved, in terminological language, for the "forces of nature" or the "force of circumstances" (*la force des choses*), that is, to indicate the energy released by physical or social movements'.[1]

---

[1] Hannah Arendt, *On Violence* (Houghton Mifflin Harcourt, Boston, MA, 1970), 45.

This is useful here: at one level, it is precisely the 'forces of nature' that, in various and extremely sophisticated ways, our physics laboratories deal with, and it is the *force des choses* – the force of circumstances – that engage our social sciences and even our humanities and arts in diverse ways. At a fundamental level, then, the university and its faculties must take an interest in force: natural force in its laboratories and material cultural and historical forces, interpersonal forces, in its libraries and seminars.

I explore here the nature of the relations that obtain between the university institution and force as such, and I examine how an interest in force relates to the other categories that interested Arendt in the study of violence that, for her in 1968, is so centred on student protest movements. I will also engage some issues regarding contemporary student movements in relation to this. Above all, however, my abiding interest is in relating the force of nature to questions of sociocultural power and authority and in how these can be articulated by a university that is avowedly worldly, in and of the material world.

Arendt was writing in the wake of student uprisings in the United States and across Europe in 1968. Those uprisings, though having various local specific inflections (such as conflicts over access to women's dormitories for male students in Nanterre), had one very specific initial fountainhead: unease with American involvement in the Vietnam War. They also had a steady supply of energy, in the students who mobilized across campus and cities in great numbers. As Patrick Seale and Maureen McConville put it in their contemporaneous book (with photographs by Chris Marker), *French Revolution 1968*:

> Students are far better equipped for insurrection that most adults recognize. They have time to plot; freedom from bread-and-butter constraints; the confidence of their class and education; faculty buildings in which to meet; above all, *energy* – the energy to march from one end of Paris to the other, to fight all night, and still be fit enough to draft, print and distribute a revolutionary tract before dawn. Adults are no match for such demonic stamina.[2]

That was in 1968. Some 50 years later, the position of the student has dramatically changed, as has the socially widespread understanding of what the university is for in a civil society. The more recent version of the student – our contemporary – has been stripped of much of this dynamic energy and force: she or he is seen increasingly as potential 'human capital', essentially as

---

[2] Seale and McConville, *French Revolution 1968* (Penguin, Harmondsworth, 1969), 71.

an operative of the systems of capital and resource management (including human resource management) in societies that are centred primarily on market economics.

The essential physical and imaginative dynamism of the Paris 1968 student has been supplanted by the dynamism of money and of a particular contemporary version of society as one based on 'growth' or what Robert and Edward Skidelsky call 'politically orchestrated insatiability' in their study of *How Much is Enough?*[3] The growth in question is measured not only by how much the individual contributes to GDP, but also by how much she or he earns in their private capacity as an employee in work. Richard Wilkinson and Kate Pickett, in *The Spirit Level*, call the belief in an axiomatic good of growth itself into question: 'Economic growth, for so long the great engine of progress, has, in the rich countries, largely finished its work'.[4] When the political establishment continue to regard growth as the foundation of all measures of the good life, we end up with 'segregation by poverty and wealth', where 'the rich are willing to pay to live separately from the poor' (p. 162), with the concomitant breakdown of the social sphere itself.

Disregarding such arguments, we now face a situation where, in succinct polemical terms, the student of today has become increasingly treated as a valuable resource (or fodder) for the ongoing smooth operations of the neo-liberal economic machinery that constitutes and governs our current 'advanced' or rich societies where economic growth has supplanted any idea of a good life as a foundation for the social or public realm. The situation, however, is not limited to advanced economies only but is also being exported and imitated elsewhere. Commenting on the United Kingdom's post-2010 'experiment' following the Browne Review's substantial step towards full privatization of the sector, Stefan Collini writes that 'the fate of British universities cannot be considered in isolation'. The pressures that the so-called 'market democracy' has put on the university are damaging British institutions, certainly, but

> unfortunately, the UK has put itself in charge of the pilot experiment [and] ... Other countries are looking on with a mixture of regret and apprehension: regret because the university system in this country has been admired for so long, apprehension because they fear similar policies may soon be coming their way.[5]

---

[3] Robert and Edward Skidelsky, *How Much is Enough?* (Penguin, London, 2013), 77.

[4] Wilkinson and Pickett, *The Spirit Level* (revised edition, Penguin, London, 2010), 5.

[5] Stefan Collini, *London Review of Books* 35: 20 (24 Oct 2013).

In the market-driven audit culture that dominates the present conception of what the university is for, students do not have 'time to plot', rather all their time is 'accounted' for. So-called continuous assessment has converted learning time into a constantly pressurized surveillance of continual examination; preparation for that examination is itself accounted for in 'contact-hour' time, which has to be maximized (quantity, being measurable, trumping quality in this). Far from being free of 'bread-and-butter' issues, student debt, constantly exacerbated by a process whereby the costs of general education of the population are transferred to individuals as personal debt, is a constantly increasing worry. To counter that, students now are increasingly part-time, given that they have to try to find paid employment simply to sustain them in their period of study. And all for what? The promised 'graduate financial dividend' may indeed be there for some, but in a world of increasingly precarious employment, many will find the economic yield less substantial than the initial investment of time and energy – or they'll join that high dream of capitalism and become the unpaid intern, or, worse still, the intern who pays for their own internship, and thus pays for the privilege of working.

The gains of modern technology are also now invading the very idea of the university as a place for people to meet, the kind of literal 'body politic' of a *collegium*. As faculty are increasingly enjoined to deploy computing technology as if it were an axiomatically good teaching-aid, lectures are podcast, seminar notes are posted on-line and, in many cases, students no longer need to be physically present as a material bodily force in a classroom. The identity of a scholarly community – a community shaped by the interplay of forces among a collective – is atomized and neutralized by the elimination of communal space and its dissolution into separate individualized cells. The classroom itself is in danger of becoming a purely virtual space, an Amazon resource that substitutes the real or historical engagement of the market with a virtual and atomized individualism: the virtual replaces the virtuous. Collegial force is dissipated through the technology, and the idea and even the very existence of a collegium, such as the students of 1968 would have known it in *le grand amphi*, the Great Amphitheatre of the Sorbonne in 1968, is diminished.

All of these changes are changes in the dynamics of force and energy, not just of individual students but also of the university itself. It is not simply the case that students have become less politically engaged – the frequent lament of *soixante-huitard* faculty; rather it is the case that the university institution, as a force within civil society, has been systematically diminished.

In 1968, however, the protests happened with a tremendous release of forceful *energy*, and they were countering the violence of US involvement in Vietnam and what was seen at the time as the incipient triumph of what

Eisenhower had christened the 'military-industrial complex'. This is the context for Arendt's writings on violence, and it is worth looking at the speech in which Eisenhower coined his resonant phrase. His speech, the last he made as US President, on 17 January 1961, delivered an austere warning.[6] He pointed out that it is only very recently that the United States had established an arms industry at all, but that the industry has grown massively, such that 'the very structure of our society' is affected by it and by the 'grave implications' that are entailed in the development of such massive technologies of force. The situation is now one where, as he put it, the 'solitary inventor' has been 'overshadowed by task forces of scientists in laboratories and testing fields'. The research required for developments in this area is so sophisticated that it has had to become intensely professionalized.

The consequence of this is that the university sector itself, as the locus of that professionalization, is radically changed. In Eisenhower's words, 'the free university, historically the fountainhead of free ideas and scientific discovery, has experienced a revolution in the conduct of research'. This revolution is one in which what we would now call 'research-grant capture' has become, in and of itself, often more important than the actual research being done: 'Partly because of the huge costs involved, a government contract becomes virtually a substitute for intellectual curiosity', he states.

Eisenhower is seeing here, somewhat prophetically, what eventually does happen in the university sector. Two things come about. First, money, in and of itself, becomes a key determinant of 'what Universities are for'. This is a kind of madness, according to Edward and Robert Skidelsky in their consideration of economics in relation to 'the good life': 'Making money cannot be an end in itself – at least for anyone not suffering from acute mental disorder' (p. 5). Secondly, government-grant capture aligns the forces of the state with the forces of the university, in ways that threaten the founding propriety of the Haldane Principle, designed to ensure that universities do not become government propaganda machines.

In the light of this emerging state of affairs, Eisenhower issues his sternest warning:

> The prospect of domination of the nation's scholars by Federal employment, project allocations, and the power of money is ever present – and is gravely to be regarded. Yet in holding scientific research and discovery in respect, as we should, we must also be alert to the equal and opposite danger that public policy could itself become the captive of a scientific-technological elite.

---

[6] Public Papers of the Presidents, Dwight D. Eisenhower, 1960, 1035–1040, available at: http://coursesa.matrix.msu.edu/~hst306/documents/indust.html.

This, very interestingly, is also close to a position adopted, much earlier, by Hannah Arendt. In 1946, she received a copy of a text written by her former mentor, Karl Jaspers, in her New York home. The text was his revised *Idea of the University*, a text rewritten and redesigned essentially to help detoxify the German tertiary sector after the atrocities of its politicization under Nazism.

Arendt admired the book, and pointed out that, given that a revived university sector would be extremely expensive, then the state should bear the costs. However, she added that, notwithstanding this, it would be good – even necessary – that the professoriate does not become civil servants. She was profoundly aware of the dangers – as had been seen under Nazism in Germany – of having a tertiary sector whose forces united with, or were forced to identify with, those of government. Indeed, article 5, section 3 of the German constitution formally enshrines the strict separation required: 'Kunst und Wissenschaft, Forschung und Lehre sind frei. Die Freiheit der Lehre entbindet nicht von der Treue zur Verfassung'. That is, 'Arts and science, research and teaching shall be free'. However, this guarantee of freedom – with subtle nicety – does not absolve the teacher or learner from the separate duties of citizenship: 'The freedom of teaching shall not release anyone from allegiance to the constitution'.

In his presidential valedictory speech, Eisenhower is aware of how the military-industrial complex can lead to a skewing of the proper relations among the government, the university and general society or culture, by eliding the separation between one's duty as a citizen and one's scholarly duty to follow where intellectual curiosity leads, and by making the latter subservient to the former. Indeed, the relation of science to government had been an abiding concern for Eisenhower. In an earlier address, given to a symposium in basic research sponsored by the National Academy of Sciences and other private organizations, and entitled 'Science: Handmaiden of Freedom', he argued that 'the search for fundamental knowledge can best be undertaken in areas and in ways determined primarily by the scientific community itself. We reject a philosophy that emphasizes more dependence upon a centralized approach and direction. Regimented research would be, for us, catastrophe'.[7] Eisenhower's presidency, at least insofar as it touched upon science and research into issues of force, is governed by the Cold War ideology that took a specific direction with the successful launch of Sputnik by the Soviet Union. Science might well have been the 'handmaiden of freedom', but it was also a key element in advancing the geopolitical position of the United States in the world.

---

[7] Available at: http://www.presidency.ucsb.edu/ws/?pid=11387.

This Cold War framework for scientific research in the mid-20th century is a clear manifestation of how 'worldly' the university needs to be. Yet, being 'worldly' does not involve a strategic political position in which communities and people are best served by direct governmental control of scientific research. Eisenhower was profoundly aware of the entire legitimacy of governmental interest in science, but, with an invocation of Tocqueville on American democracy, he also argues not only that science should be returned to the primary determinations of intellectual curiosity, but also that this should be done in the interests of good democratic citizenship.

In practice, then, one aspect of the student revolts of which Arendt writes in 1968 – revolts whose archaeological prehistory goes back to the Cold War and its confrontation of different ideologies – is shaped by an attempt to recall the university to what, in mid-20th century, was seen by some as its proper activity, of engaging force in ways that eschew its deviation into violence – war – within and between cultures. The challenge issued by the students of 1968 was to become a direct challenge to state authority.

The difference is that such a position is virtually and constitutionally impossible now; so great has been the capture of the university's force by the overpowering and overbearing force of the state. Eisenhower's caution and warnings have been ignored. Successive governments, of all political persuasions, have arrogated to themselves the right to determine the nature and direction of research and teaching, and successive Quisling sector leaders, self-styled 'CEOs', 'Presidents' and Vice-Chancellors, have been quick to acquiesce, spying either personal advancement or advancement of their own institution over others, gained through their supine compliance with state power. However, it is no longer the intimacy of the university with military force that is at issue in the present state of affairs, rather the intimacy of the university is now forged with economic forces, to the detriment of its social responsibilities and authority.

Arendt defines authority as something that can be vested in persons or institutions. The institutional example she offers first is that of the Roman senate, and, in such cases,

> the hallmark of authority 'is unquestioning recognition by those who are asked to obey; neither coercion nor persuasion is needed ... To remain in authority requires respect for the person or the office. The greatest enemy of authority, therefore, is contempt, and the surest way to undermine it is laughter.' (Arendt 1970, p. 45)

And, in 1968, as Seale and McConville pointed out, Daniel Cohn-Bendit 'turned clowning into a punishing political weapon. Totally unimpressed by age, rank, or authority – by all the protective cant of the adult world – his talent was to keep a mocking finger pointed at the Emperor's testicles' (p. 57). While Eisenhower's world was dominated by the fear of nuclear tragedy, Cohn-Bendit was able to see the power of comedy as a political weapon – and to reclaim the university as a site not for catastrophe but for criticism and for play, for provisionality. Yet, just two years later, on 4 May 1970, the university found itself again at the centre of an issue of force, not in Paris but in Ohio. That day, troopers from the Ohio Army National Guard fired on students in Kent State University, killing four and wounding another nine. This event yielded one of the most iconic images of the period, John Filo's photograph of Jeffrey Miller, one of the four dead, with Mary-Anne Vecchio crying out beside his corpse. 'Tin soldiers and Nixon coming, we're finally on our own', sang Neil Young with CSNY. State violence here crushed the authority of a protesting student body. Such confrontations are, in our own time, becoming increasingly common, even if less dramatic than a situation involving firearms and death. 'Cops on campus' are increasingly visible as a means by which university authorities seek to quash protest, dissent or criticism, and violence crushes play.

Our guiding question here is about the authority of the university, and I explore how that authority might be gleaned from the engagement with primary force. Two things will be of special importance: first, the question of the proper separation of mission or purpose as between university and state (what we might call the forces of circumstance or the place of the university, as a worldly institution, in the public and social sphere); second, the ways in which this worldly university engages primarily and crucially with the forces of nature, or with what is described at one point in Shakespeare's *Coriolanus* as the 'sovereignty of nature'. The year 1968 was partly shaped by attitudes to war, and specifically to US involvement in Vietnam, at least in terms of the worldly political dimensions of student protest. It is appropriate, then, in a development of some observations laid out in my *Introduction* chapter, to consider how the Great War helped shape the origins of the modern and contemporary university, and it is to this that I now turn.

1.2 TYRANTS IN THE MARKET OR FINANCIAL VIOLENCE

The French thinker and poet, Paul Valéry, thought about these issues, though not explicitly in terms of the university institution; he thought about them in terms of the relation of civilization to the violence that is endemic in war and in a wartime economy and environment. In April 1919, he sent two letters (published as *La Crise de l'Esprit: or Crisis of the Mind*) to *The Athenaeum*, a literary journal based in London, that was modernist, internationalist and broadly liberal in political outlook. He was writing from Paris in the immediate aftermath of the Great War, which would turn out to be but the first of a series that caused terrible destruction, especially to the civilizations of Europe.

The letters begin with a stark statement about the fundamental fragility of civilizations. The very opening sentence of the first letter states the position clearly. Like the character of Hamlet who will later play a key role in the letters, Valéry holds a skull before us and gives us a *memento mori*: 'Nous autres, civilisations, nous savons maintenant que nous sommes mortelles' (we, the civilized, now know that we too are mortal).[8] In the wake of the Great War, we now know that civilizations are themselves as fragile and precarious as the life of an individual human being. The letters are framed by an insistence on this precariousness, by an awareness that what we know as civilization has at least one disconcerting trouble: it may be merely a transitory historical state of affairs and is no protection against the flow of change, the secular dimensions of historical mutability that can allow others, through force, to assume violent or authoritarian superiority in world affairs.

The central argument of the letters derives from Valéry's 'fundamental theorem' regarding civilization and the world system or world order. That theorem states that the world is fundamentally predisposed to inequality and that this inequality derives from physical forces that are themselves given by basic geography and population demographics. Some parts of the world are more richly endowed than others in natural resources. They have a more fertile soil, a subsoil containing more valuable minerals, a landmass that is well irrigated, an infrastructure that makes transport and the like easier, greater population numbers and thus greater force and strength and so on. There is, as it were, a natural inequality across the world's regions and that inequality is intrinsically governed by – and potentially guaranteed by – the primacy of the forces of nature or what Adam Smith had thought of as the logic of 'natural advantage'.

The planet, argues Valéry, can be described at any given instant in terms of this play of unequal forces. It is a terminology that we might now be more readily familiar with under the developments in geography and other disciplines that depend on an understanding of what Trotsky called 'uneven and combined development'. Interestingly, then, it seems clear that through the tumultuous events of the latter half of the 1910s, not just in Europe but also in revolutionary Russia, there developed a profound awareness of intrinsic inequalities as a fundamental problem or issue for the world order. It is perhaps

---

[8] Text available at: http://classiques.uqac.ca/classiques/Valery_paul/crise_de_lesprit/valery_esprit.pdf.

not surprising, then, that the discipline of 'International Relations' (IR) began, properly, as a university discipline also in 1919.

That disciplinary beginning has its roots precisely in the Paris Peace Conference that ended the Great War and helped establish the League of Nations. One great supporter of the League of Nations was David Davies, Liberal MP for Montgomeryshire in Wales, who (with his sisters, Gwendoline and Margaret) endowed the first university professorship in IR (named for Woodrow Wilson), in the University of Aberystwyth. IR as a discipline brings the question of geopolitical force right into the heart of the university in the early 20th century, and it does so in a way that tries to regulate the relations between the forces of nature on one hand (geographical terrain) and the force of circumstance on the other (governmental policy – especially foreign policy – based in organizations of nation states).

Yet, asks Valéry, how is it that if the theorem is right, we find that Europe, which is less well-endowed and less massively populated than elsewhere in the world, nonetheless finds itself in the first rank of strength and development in the world? IR would have talked about 'power' in response to this. Valéry's answer lies in what he describes, less philosophically or theoretically – and in terms that the present day would find rather suspect – as the 'European psyche'. The description that he offers of this psyche is interesting for its proximity to those characteristics that are often associated with the institution of the university. He describes its qualities: a burning but disinterested curiosity, a scepticism that is not pessimistic, an attention to mystery that does not resign itself to unknowing and eager aspiration for progress. He proceeds to offer a specific single example: Greece, the site of the foundation of *geometry*.

This is where we get to the absolute core of Valéry's argument, and also to the centre of why it is so important for our contemporary understanding of the relation of force to the university. Geometry, a science that begins from the measuring of the earth itself as a physical entity, allows for the very exploration of space itself, and at every level, not just physical space (its primary concern) but also, through this, the spatial organization of virtually all of the components of knowledge itself. Geometry *organizes* otherwise random forces and allows us to find and essentially to control physical space and the human lived environment through the deployment of definitions, axioms, theorems and even the fundamental lexical and syntactic organizations of languages in which we find the possibilities of proofs. Even grammar – the foundation of our mutual social cooperation through language and understanding – is a kind of subset of geometry, and, as Philippe Sollers would claim in the wake of 1968, 'grammar is already a question of the police' and thus related directly (if jocularly) to the polity.

The domain of scientific knowledge, then, is where we find a way of allowing the intellect to engage with force, in such a way that brute force – the natural order of inequalities – does not necessarily hold sway. In fact, the balance of powers between Europe (in this case) and the rest of the naturally more forceful world is swayed entirely by the triumph of what Valéry now associates with civilizational force itself, the force that we might recognize as that of the university. The intellectual activity – here, that of Greek geometry – acts as a counter to the otherwise unequal celebration of mere physical force or violence: it counters the ideology of 'might is right'. Geometry is to the classical world, then, what IR is to the modern. We can put forward the crude analogy here: the university exists to counter social, economic and political inequalities of brute natural force, and it does so through the kinds of abstract thought that govern the operations of geometry.

In 1919, however, this was not the whole story for Valéry. Science and its achievements are not necessarily always good but are often subject to laws of unintended consequences. The horrors that he had just witnessed in the war are not just the result of some simplistic prevalence of evil; rather what happened is that positively good intentions (hard work, solid principles of discipline and so on) were turned to bad ends through some fundamental perversion of their intrinsic qualities – that is, by accident and not by design.

To be sure, wrote Valéry, science must have made great progress: 'Il a fallu, sans doute, beaucoup de science pour tuer tant d'hommes, dissiper tant de biens, anéantir tant de villes en si peu de temps' ('we needed a great deal of science, surely, to kill so many men, destroy so many goods, annihilate so many towns in such little time'; p. 4). The real struggle, as he sees it, is not so much whether science is an intrinsic good as much as whether it addresses properly the issue of unequal natural forces, the 'sovereignty of nature'. It is less a question of whether science should be in the dock and more a question of the relation of science (vested here in Valéry's 'European psyche') to the intrinsic inequalities that the world's natural resources and geopolitical conditions give us. That is to say, how can science counter the fundamental force of superior numbers, superior natural resources that make the world a potentially unequal place, a place condemned to organize itself through bullying force? For us, here, now the same question persists, but with the wider frame of reference: how might the university counter the potentially negative effects whereby nature – or an ideology that presents itself as 'natural' – holds sway over us by some basic and crude force?

Further, Valéry is troubled not just by this fundamental issue, but even more by how he sees it actually playing out in 1919. Given what he had described as the fragility and secular mutability of civilizations (we will all die), he is now profoundly aware, after 1919, that what we had seen as the supremacy of geometry is, like many good scientific things, leading to bad ends. Valéry points out that once we have realized the power of geometry, it changes its own nature. Geometry allowed, in its application, for a means whereby science becomes power: science becomes a means of domination that in turn yields great wealth and allows for an exploitation of the entire planet. At this point, geometry has stopped being 'an end in itself' and 'an artistic activity'. Rather, now, knowledge – which had been a value in terms of its own accomplishment or, as we would more conventionally put it, an end in itself – became instead a *commodity*, desirable not just to a select few but also across the entire world.

This – knowledge transformed into stable commodity – thereby changes its own intrinsic nature and form and becomes a thing marketized: 'elle deviendra chose du Commerce, chose enfin qui s'imite et se produit un peu partout' ('it was to become a matter of Commerce, an imitable product available everywhere'). In short, knowledge becomes a business proposition, something for sale across a wide market in the world. This is the start of a supposed 'knowledge-economy' which, in this bare form, reveals itself for what it is: knowledge inserted into world economies in marketable form as a series of commodities: more simply put, information and data for sale or rent. In its extreme and somewhat perverted form, we know this as the metadata that has become the currency of surveillance for those arms of state called 'security services', like the NSA or GCHQ.

Now, we should be clear that the widespread deployment of knowledge is not itself the problem, rather the problem is that, thus widespread and equally shared *through its commodification and marketization*, the very force that gave Europe its superiority over the primacy of natural force, with its intrinsic tendency to bullying and coercion, no longer has that countervailing power. When the whole world shares this same geometry, a geometry no longer identified with intellect (or civil society) but with market-wealth (or commercialization), then we return to that prior state of affairs whereby those who have more natural resources (in this case, individual wealth) reassert their own fundamental force.

Robert and Edward Skidelsky indicate what is wrong-headed in this. The primacy of money as a major determinant of social life, they say, troubled Aristotle – and troubles them – because of 'its power to subordinate the proper end of every human activity to the ancillary end of money-making' (p. 75). This yields the corruptions that we know only too well in contemporary societies: 'doctors think only of their fee; soldiers fight only for pay; sophists trade wisdom for gain' (p. 75). Further, money breeds insatiability:

Use-values have ... a controlling end: the good life. To pursue them beyond this point is senseless. Money, by contrast, has no controlling end ... Money is the one thing of which there is never enough, for the simple reason that the concept 'enough' has no logical application to it (p. 75).

Those UK vice chancellors (but they are not alone; this is not a solely UK-based phenomenon) who have been awarding themselves extravagant salaries may know the full meaning of this. In 2014, while limiting academic pay increases to a maximum of 1%, some have awarded themselves pay raises of 22% or, in one extreme case, 39%. This latter represented a pay rise of some £105,000, or roughly four times the full annual average UK salary. These are being awarded not only to VCs who claim that they cannot afford to pay academics any more, but also to VCs who keep newly emerging PhD-holding academics to zero-hours contracts, hourly rates that are significantly below the national minimum wage, and who outsource support staff, transferring them to private-sector companies who give them a free option: accept even lower pay, or lose your job. There are, of course, honourable exceptions among the United Kingdom's VCs, but they are, indeed, exceptional. In some cases, as Aditya Chakraborrty points out, the increases are precisely like those awarded to the bankers post-2008: rewards for failure.[9] Just as the banks ruined economies by 'diversifying' and growing too big to fail, so universities, thinking of themselves as commercial businesses, lose sight of their primary and central activities. The result is inequality that scars the sector as a whole and calls into question the primacy of the economic and financial force that clearly threatens to corrupt the university.

Finance, or individual wealth, now becomes the key and determining force, and it is a force that has co-opted its countervailing authority, that of civilization or, tragically, of the university.

I noted above that geometry was to the ancient world what IR is to the modern. Here, there is a further comparison available: geometry is to the ancient world as *oil* and similar resources are to the modern. Oil, as one of the most important natural resources in the contemporary environment, threatens the world order with not only war but also the resulting mass inequalities against which mere intellect cannot fight back. The ownership of oil, as well as of gas and even water, is increasingly in the hands of either private companies or individual oligarchs: this is the logic of neo-liberal 'privatization'. It is also a

---

[9] See http://www.theguardian.com/commentisfree/2014/mar/03/new-breed-fat-cats-university-boss-vice-chancellors. What we are seeing here is the dying embers of an unsustainable greed, as CEOs, in virtually all sectors, grab what they can, knowing that the neo-liberal greed game might well be up.

geopolitical condition that governs conflict, as we have seen in Iraq, Ukraine and elsewhere. In the Middle East, the appropriation of land through occupied settlements is vital as a source of underground water in a parched desert environment.

The world of privatized utilities is generative of anti-civil attitudes. And, as it is with actual worldly political conditions, so also it is with institutional conditions within the polity, including the privatizing and commercialization of knowledge within and through the university. As Shakespeare has it, we are in a position where ancient grudges are reborn, where 'civil blood makes civil hands unclean' or where 'The blood-dimmed tide is loosed', as Yeats had it in 'The Second Coming', a poem more or less contemporaneous with Valéry's letters.

In this state of affairs, Valéry asks, is the European spirit amenable to being spread more generally, without detriment to those – like those in Europe – who are weak in natural or physical force, weak in natural resources and smaller in mass numbers? Is there any freedom to act against the threat of an establishment of inequality based on force? The answer he offers returns us to the fundamental task of what we would now call research: 'it is perhaps by seeking this freedom that we create it'; and the search will involve a study, within the thinking individual, of 'the struggle between the personal and the social life'.

This is a fundamental struggle for a specific kind of democracy, as outlined by John Stuart Mill. Mill feared the 'tyranny of the majority', and he tried to answer it with a strict separation of individual personal desire and the social good. As he put it in *On Liberty*, 'To individuality should belong the part of life in which it is chiefly the individual that is interested; to society, the part which chiefly interests society'[10]. The predicament of force, as it concerns us, is thus also an issue regarding democracy, and the marketization of knowledge is one of our world's greatest threats to democracy.

Clearly, Valéry's anxieties have some contemporary counterparts, and they also speak of some contemporary issues. He wrote in the wake of war, and we now find ourselves discussing the future of the university in an allegedly globalized environment, but one where the greatest global experience might well be quite simply that of war itself. The contemporary wars are also, fundamentally, wars over natural resources, be it water in the Middle East, or oil in Iraq and after, or the resources, controlled by multinational corporate entities, to feed a burgeoning world population. In the face of this, issues around democracy have become crucial, and it is crucial that the contemporary worldly university finds some way of engaging these issues. What is or should be the relation of a

---

[10] Mill, *On Liberty* (Penguin, London, 2006), 132.

centre of alleged civilization, or at least of civil society, to the violent destruction of cities, of traditions and of cultural forms and practices? How can we find a means of countering the prevailing tendencies to govern by force: either direct physical force in tyrannous jurisdictions or the indirect coercive force of market-poverty and structural inequalities of wealth?

We might re-position the terms of Valéry's argument. We might pose the question of whether the university – as an institution that is central to civil society in real and material terms – can or should be a bulwark against not just crude force but also against larger and world-scale uneven development. If so, then the university essentially can become a force for the growth of various kinds of equality, an institution whose guiding principles might be shaped by a desire to counter the hierarchies that are yielded by the accidents of physical force or the accidents of geopolitical circumstance (*la force des choses*). This would entail an exploration of the place of the institutions of knowledge in a world polity that is increasingly dominated by economics, and by an economics whose neo-liberal version is guided by a necessary but destabilizing growth in inequality. Such a growth in inequality is one that some conservative thinking wants to identify precisely as 'natural', a kind of genetic *force of nature*, opposition to which or even criticism of which must appear 'unnatural' and thus also even unspeakable, intrinsically monstrous.

In sum, how is it that the university, characterized as an institution driven by the primacy of demands for knowledge, addresses the politics of force in the contemporary material world? In asking this, we need to learn not just from the contemporary moment of uneven developments that describe only some privileged parts of the global environment as 'civilized', but also from previous civil societies and previous explorations of force and learning. Given, further, the clear relevance of Mill's anxieties about the potential tyranny of the majority that lurks within representative democracies, we also need to find ways of addressing the proper relation between education as a matter of individual and personal interest and education as a worldly public good for civil society.

For this, we can turn to the illustrative example of Shakespeare's *Coriolanus*, a play that seems preoccupied with the potential emergence of democratic power set against ruling patrician privilege. It is here that we see a key political exploration of the politics of natural force, the 'sovereignty of nature'.

1.3 ENTITLEMENT AND THE RIGHT TO THE UNIVERSITY

At issue is a contestation between the authority of force on one hand against the authority of civil society on the other hand. This is an issue concerning democracy. What is the relation of the university to civil authority? From whom does it derive its cultural standing and authority, its 'rights to the city', its right to speak in the polity or its right to speak truth to power? What is it that 'entitles' the university as an institution and that gives it an authoritative name and identity? How, in short, does an institution of learning get the authority to call itself a university?

This is the world that Shakespeare explores in one of his most pertinent Roman plays, *Coriolanus*, performed for the first time roughly in 1607, and perhaps coincident with England's 'Midlands Revolts'. These were essentially struggles between landlords who enclosed and privatized land and commoners who gathered together in protest, levelling the enclosure hedges and so on. What was at issue in those revolts was fundamentally 'a political struggle over the constitution of authority in the countryside'[11].

At one level, the play is fundamentally about 'entitlement', and about who should have cultural and political entitlement to power and rule. On one hand, Caius Marcius is literally 'entitled', as he is renamed to become Coriolanus. On the other hand, as the play makes clear, are not the people of the city themselves entitled to food, when it is in abundance, and are they not also entitled to their voices and votes, in order to underpin civic or civil authority in the figure of Coriolanus? This is the opening of *Coriolanus*, essentially: a people up in arms against a patrician Roman authority, the people lacking bread while the patricians revel in abundance, 1607's version of the 99% and the 1% so succinctly described in our time by the economist Joseph Stiglitz. There is, as it were, a massive structural inequality with respect to resources. This situation exemplifies what Stiglitz calls 'the price of inequality' and its attendant problems, when he points out that 'Countries rich in natural resources are infamous for rent-seeking activities',[12] and *Coriolanus* was set in precisely such an economics.

Coriolanus himself is a clear manifestation of brute physical or natural force. He fights entire armies alone and vanquishes them. He is a manifestation of the 'sovereignty of nature', to borrow a pregnant phrase from the lexicon of his great enemy and rival, Tullus Aufidius. Yet he is also a pure force that becomes mythologized through his literal 'entitlement' as seen in his new name 'Coriolanus'. The play, however, is one that is written partly to examine the very idea of such patrician and mythological entitlement, for it plays with an emergent idea of democracy.

Against Coriolanus, we find the ranked masses of 'the people', who proclaim their own entitlement by trying to reclaim the streets. 'What is the city

---

[11] Victor V. Magagna, *Communities of Grain: Rural Rebellion in Comparative Perspective* (Cornell University Press, New York, 1991), 120.

[12] Stiglitz, *The Price of Inequality* (Penguin, London, 2013), 49.

but the people', asks Sicinius, the Tribune in Act 3, scene 1, and the people reply, chanting together that 'The people are the city'. The contemporary version of this chant and statement is to be found in the Occupy movement. In *Rebel Cities*, David Harvey asserts the claims of Occupy Wall Street ('it is we who are the public') against the forces of 'mayors, police chiefs, military officers, and state officials'.[13] The Rome of *Coriolanus* is just one such 'rebel city', an enclosure or privatized space whose ownership and legitimate occupation is being challenged by its people.

In Shakespeare's time, we should recall, 'Empire' did not mean 'British Empire'. Historically, and as we know from the plays, it probably meant something to do with empires that were centred – as for the much later Valéry – somewhere in the Mediterranean. For Valéry, it was a necessity to place the entire shoreline of the Mediterranean in Europe (Smyrna and Alexandria are as much European as are Athens and Marseilles, he argued). If we turn to Shakespeare, we find an interesting state of affairs in this 'centre of the Earth', this world-centre.

Braudel showed how the entire Mediterranean goes into a state of some turmoil after about 1589, with a crisis in France and a crisis across Islam. The death of Henri III provoked, in the region, anxieties specifically about trade: the stories coming out of France were doing real damage to trade, according to Braudel. Meanwhile, following the death of the Turkish ruler, Euldj Ali, in 1587, there was, all across the Islamic Mediterranean, 'une crise d'autorité turque', a parallel crisis of Turkish authority.[14]

There is a European crisis (fundamentally associated with trade), and there is a crisis in Islam that spreads across North Africa from the East (Braudel 1993, p. 360). During this period, contemporaneous with the writing of the play, a kind of proto-Arab Spring was happening across North Africa, contributing to fundamentally financial anxieties on the northern borders of the Mediterranean. When Shakespeare thought of empire, it is these empires and not anything specifically 'British' that he had in mind. Perhaps above all, when he thought of the centre of the world's power and gravity, he turned to the empire that was Rome, and, given the history in whose midst he sat, the view of Rome that is culturally 'available' to him was one where there was specifically a crisis of geopolitical power. That crisis is, in turn, shaped by the emerging modern nations around the Mediterranean shoreline and their taste for the acquisition of the world's natural resources (especially silver), the satisfactions of which depended upon authoritative command of the seas.

---

[13] Harvey, *Rebel Cities* (Verso, London, 2013), 163.

[14] Braudel, *La Méditerranée et le monde méditerranéen*, vol 3 (Livre de Poche, Paris, 1993), 358, 361.

It is these same power structures that govern today's contemporary version of the question of 'entitlement' and its relation to privilege or to self-serving elites. At stake here is a two-fold question: who 'commands' the forces of nature that shape our world and what is the relation of the university – with its concerns for research, knowledge and thinking – to such material force? What is it that entitles the university to exert a power or authority over brute force? In *Coriolanus*, the question is put directly: what entitles the people to exert authority over the force of nature that is Coriolanus? The answer is also put directly, if controversially: their collective poverty, stemming from the intrinsic inequalities of Rome. It is inequality such as this that legitimizes their revolt, and it is the drive for inequality that leads Coriolanus eventually to the corruption of a fundamental treachery when he proposes to help Tullus Aufidius to sack Rome itself.

Our contemporary world order rehearses a similar series of Mediterranean crises as those described by Braudel in the late 16th century. In nearly all the countries bordering the Mediterranean, there has been a crisis of democracy, occasioned by finance, poverty and the extreme form of inequality that goes by the name of dictatorship (along the southern shores) or technocracy (in the north). Appropriately enough for this present chapter, during Greece's more recent post-2008 financial crisis, Jean-Luc Godard indicated the massive debt that the world owes to Greece. Greece gave us, he said, the word 'donc' – *therefore* – the very logic or geometry that allows us to think logically that 'if P, therefore Q'. Accordingly, and with his characteristic half-joking-whole-serious flourish reminiscent of the impudent clowning of a Cohn-Bendit, and more seriously recalling to our mind Valéry's crisis of the spirit, he argued that we should donate €1 to Greece every time we utter the word 'donc'.

Geometry gives us the birth of modern science (it gives authority, method, verification and so on). Its central determination is to give a form to force, to take the crude banality of physical force and to find a means of containing it and even of countering it. Following my discussion above, it would be a comfort to be able to say that the university is properly the institution that exists to counter the primacy of force in the world, to ensure that 'might' does not necessarily become 'right' simply by coercive violence and threat of domination. The story is more complicated, however – else we would have the solace of arguing that the university can solve the geopolitical problems of the post-9/11 world. Sadly, it is not that straightforward.

In his great foundational text of post-structuralism, 'Force and Signification', Derrida points out that '*Form* fascinates when one no longer has the force to understand force from within itself. That is, to create'.[15] Essentially, geometry

---

[15] Derrida, *Writing and Difference* (trans. Alan Bass; University of Chicago Press, 1980), 4–5.

lurks behind a criticism that now is troubled by its own inefficacy, a criticism that 'knows itself separated from force' and that celebrates instead its own 'technical ingenuity or mathematical subtlety' (Derrida 1980, p. 5). Commerce, in its commodification of knowledge – or the mathematical subtleties of banking's 'credit-default swaps' or 'sub-primes' and the algorithms that have wrecked large parts of the world economy – is precisely one such attempt to 'contain' knowledge itself or to restrict it and its efficacy for change.

Commerce gives a form to intellectual force in this sense, and thereby precludes creativity. It replaces creativity with consumerism and homogenization, or that false form of 'equality' that simply acts as a cover for the triumph of physical or financial force: money. Georg Simmel, in his *Philosophy of Money*, worried precisely about the homogenizing and 'flattening' power of money, which reduced 'the concrete values of life' to abstract form and to what he called 'the mediating value of money'. In mediating all things, money 'equates' value with price, but it does so to the detriment of things to be as they are: unique and specific.[16]

Knowledge, in the triumph of a geometry that brought wealth and equalized the world's uneven powers, was itself a specific kind of force. However, when knowledge is commercialized, subsumed under the form of commerce and commodity, we get an instrumentalization of knowledge that dissociates knowledge from all that is civil or civilizing. Instead, such commercialized 'formal' knowledge starts to exacerbate precisely those inequalities that it might otherwise counter.

In short, to put this into the terminology that we have already seen explored in Arendt, knowledge becomes not power but strength: '*Strength* unequivocally designates something in the singular, an individual entity; it is the property inherent in an object or person and belongs to its character' (Arendt 1970, p. 44). By contrast, '*Power* corresponds to the human ability not just to act but to act in concert. Power is never the property of an individual; it belongs to a group and remains in existence only so long as the group keeps together' (Arendt 1970, p. 44).

If, as the cliché has it, 'knowledge is power', then knowledge has to be non-commercial, nor-marketable: social.

1.4 THE CORRUPTING OF DEMOCRACY

Let us be explicit about the question at issue here. It is more than the usual question that is cast in terms of the social role, or social mission, of the university.

---

[16] Simmel, *Money; Philosophie des Geldes*, 1900; (trans. Tom Bottomore and David Frisby; Routledge, London, 1978), 255.

It is more fundamental than this. For Bill Readings, writing in 1994, the 'wider social role of the university is now up for grabs'.[17] Now, however, we have to realize that that mission has indeed been 'grabbed': the university has been co-opted to a specific role, and it is one where the civil society itself has lost out. In what we might call a *coup de force*, the university itself has been weakened, its democratic credentials largely discarded and disengaged, and its large social, ethical and political responsibilities reduced and shrunk into bureaucratic 'accountabilities' in an economic structure that dispenses with any notion of a worldly ecology of learning, thought and criticism.

When François Mitterrand launched his attack in 1964 on what he saw as the unauthorized claims to power that General De Gaulle was amassing to himself through a centralization of power in the person of 'De Gaulle', he was addressing the same fundamental problem that we saw in *Coriolanus*. What Mitterrand saw as a *coup d'état permanent* is entirely akin to the *coup de force* in which the university and its potential for democracy is weakened. Further, Mitterrand's polemic in 1964 is itself instrumental not just in shaking De Gaulle, but also in laying some of the ground for the student revolts just four years later.

Further, and baldly stated, in this *coup*, the university has become an instrument for advancing and furthering inequalities of wealth, presenting such inequalities as 'natural', and thereby disqualifying anything critical of such a position as 'unnatural'. In its most extreme forms, it is not just critical thinking that is now to be penalized, but yet more fundamentally, the very activity of thinking itself. Now, even the very activity of thinking about the conditions of civilization or of worldliness – as opposed to merely efficiently operating a pre-existing and allegedly 'natural' state of economic and political affairs – is precisely what is described as 'alien' or unnatural. 'I think, therefore I am dangerous'.

If thinking is at the core of a university, then we are now witnessing an attack on the fundamental principles of the university, the like of which we have never seen before, going beyond any mere iconoclasm or barbarism. What makes this situation worse is that, as in the Trojan War, the enemy is to be found already within the gates: there is virtually no official countervailing argument or defence launched from within the institution itself. Any such defence is intrinsically de-legitimized because it is axiomatically 'unnatural' – which now simply means unorthodox.

In his study, *Violence*, Slavoj Žižek points out that violence is an essential constituent of what we might call our sociocultural ecology. Violence is, in fact, that state of affairs or condition in which *talk about* our environment

---

[17] Bill Readings, *The University in Ruins* (Harvard University Press, 1994), 2.

(ecology) is transformed into *laws governing* our environment (economy). This is not quite how Žižek puts it, but his argument helps explain the position I am outlining here.

The governing idea in Žižek's *Violence* is that what we often call violence in our societies is simply the visible portion of a larger-scale 'objective' violence that does not usually reveal itself. This objective violence – a violence that is not just, and maybe not even, a matter of perception or the aesthetics of violence – is grounded in two things. The first (which will concern us less here) is the 'symbolic' violence 'embodied in language' (whereby language itself imposes 'a certain universe of meaning' or delimits what it is possible to think: Sollers' grammar as a 'question of the police'). The second is more important for present purposes. This is what Žižek calls 'systemic' violence: 'the often catastrophic consequences of the smooth functioning of our economic and political systems'.[18]

The university, as a site for engaging the forces that constitute and even sustain the world, cannot afford to ignore its relation to those forces and to this systemic violence. My contention is that the university is that institution that has a responsibility to counter the incipient violence of natural force with a view to ensuring that our world does not suffer from the unequal distribution of strength that derives from happenstance geography, or from inequalities given by individual wealth. Further, it is an institution among whose central purposes is to act as a bulwark against natural force as such – bullying – with a view to reducing inequality more generally.

These arguments place the university at the centre of an ecology. This is slightly different from the arguments recently advanced by Ron Barnett, when he puts forward an idea of what he calls a 'becoming-university' institution that is governed by a quasi-Heideggerian 'care or concern' towards its local and global 'networks' of engagement. This 'feasible utopia', as Barnett calls it, is dedicated towards a flowering of imagination.[19] This is necessary, certainly, but what I am arguing for is something that I think is yet more fundamental.

An ecology is, by definition, a means of understanding our home: an *oikos* shaped by *logos*, a home environment that is understood by how we talk about it, even about how we shape it through the prioritizations of our most important meanings and meaningful activities. What we have witnessed in recent decades across both the developed and developing worlds is a fundamental act of *reduction*. 'Ecology' has been overtaken by 'economy': a home environment or *oikos* that is now governed not by talk or discussion, but instead by *law*, by *nomos*. This seems to raise the stakes and importance of ecology, and

---

[18] Slavoj Žižek, *Violence* (Profile Books, London, 2009), 1.

[19] Ron Barnett, *Being a University* (Routledge, Abingdon, 2011), 142.

to do so in ways that are normatively associated with the intellectual work of a university. The institution's task, we have often thought (especially in bourgeois liberal circles), is to establish normative laws that govern how we understand and engage with the world around us. This, indeed, is what Readings once called 'the university of culture', that Humboldtian version of the university that proposed norms for a nation's citizenship while also producing the very citizens capable of living up to those norms.

However, at the same time, the laws in question are, in modernity, fundamentally simply financial: the law and all its processes of legislation are governed by money. This yields what we have recently seen: a state of affairs in which democracy itself is skewed by finance. We no longer have the democracy of 'one person, one vote', but rather, as Stiglitz points out, a democracy grounded in the logic of 'one dollar, one vote'. Stiglitz cites a 2010 decision in the US courts (the case is referred to as that of 'Citizens United *versus* Federal Election Commission'). In the judgement on this case, 'the Supreme Court essentially approved unbridled corporate campaign spending', which Stiglitz describes as 'a milestone in the disempowerment of ordinary Americans' (Stiglitz 2013, p. 165). Legislation protecting 'free speech' in this case actually means empowering the speech of those who, with the largest budgets, can drown out the financially less well-endowed. Money talks, citizens don't.

This casts a helpful light on what is, by now, a standard 'realistic' position about the university's relation to public policy. Like many soi-disant realistic positions, this one essentially is rather quietist, desperate and expressive of a tacit solidarity with coercive 'public opinion': a state of affairs that is neither an opinion nor genuinely public, and which Christopher Hitchens memorably described, in a debate with Shashi Tharoor in 2007, as 'the greatest threat to free expression'.[20] The claim of 'realism' is actually simply an excuse for preservation of the status quo, for it rests on the assumption that what is 'realistic' is, by definition, that which really exists at the present time. Thus, anything that is critical – anything that thinks otherwise, or that even thinks at all – is inherently unrealistic. The net result is that those who are currently in a position of power remain in that position, and 'realism' is their guarantee that their power will be perpetual. Thus it is that power trumps legitimate authority every time, for power regards legitimate authority – based on reason, argument or debate and serious critical thinking – as unrealistic fantasy. As such, legitimate authority, based in democratic argument, can safely be ignored. Power, within the university sector, now never feels the need to justify itself: it just is. 'This is this'. In this respect, it is like the finance industries.

---

[20] See http://www.youtube.com/watch?v=jw3dDbc1BHE.

This kind of position is laid out by William Melody in an essay on 'Universities and Public Policy', published in 1997, in a collection quizzically entitled *The Postmodern University?* There, Melody rightly indicated in 1997 was what turned out to be an accurate prediction of a general political trajectory over the next two decades. This traces the demise of an idealistic version of the university as an institution that disinterestedly searches for truth in various domains. That institution is increasingly replaced by an institution that 'serves' (or carries out the will of) its funding masters, identified in the UK sector usually as 'government'. Money talks, and government now is itself governed by money. As the 2008 crisis showed worldwide, banks were able – and, indeed, remain able – to hold entire governments and peoples to ransom.[21]

These governments, of course, though democratically elected, find quickly that their programmes are nonetheless shaped largely by private interest groups and their lobbyists, so that government departments increasingly 'make decisions based primarily on assessments of research prepared to support advocacy positions being presented by different special interests' (Melody, p. 77). The reduction of government funding for universities, paradoxically, goes hand-in-hand with an increase in governmental regulation of the institutions and their activities, but that regulation is itself shaped by the demands not of 'the public' – citizens – but rather of special private sector business and associated interests: 'Government is more and more the negotiating arena for special interests, and less and less the representative of the broader societal issues, those that are common to everyone but not the specific responsibility of anyone' (Melody, 77).

This is consistent with Stiglitz's observation that, in the United States, political decisions in Congress are increasingly driven by money, and by the 1% that holds most of it. He writes that in Congress, 'there are more than 3,100 lobbyists working for the health industry (nearly 6 for every congressperson), and 2,100 lobbyists working for the energy and natural resources industries. All told, more than $3.2bn was spent on lobbying in 2011 alone'. Similarly, in the United Kingdom in 2013, the lobbying industry was worth some £2bn.

We should note that a substantial part of this lobbying is done on behalf of precisely those energy industries and natural resources whose geopolitical enclosure is responsible for the forced and force-based inequalities of the world that gave Valéry his fundamental theorem a century ago. Let us not forget that John Browne, chair of the United Kingdom's 2010 Browne Review, had been chairman of BP, responsible for its massive expansion which many argue came

---

[21] See Antony Smith and Frank Webster, eds., *The Postmodern University?* (Open University Press, Buckingham, 1997), 72–84.

at the cost of maintaining safety and therefore led to the Deepwater Horizon oil spill of 2010. Further, the lobbying in question has succeeded in ensuring that government-funded university research and teaching increasingly supplement and even replace private sector financing of R&D costs. This is the kind of thing that Stiglitz refers to as 'corporate welfare', and the 'realistic' sector leadership in tertiary education has increasingly been complicit in what is essentially a systematic transfer of commonly-shared wealth into the hands of a few private sector interests or individuals.

In the so-called 'developing' world, this is called 'corruption'. In the so-called 'advanced' economies, it is called realism.

Melody doesn't simply analyse the problems; he also proposes, as a solution, that the university take upon itself a role in trying to shape public policy. This, too, has come about, but in highly muted and co-opted form. It is what is known, especially or primarily in the United Kingdom, as 'the impact agenda', in which the university has to make clear, audit-style, how the research that it does increases GDP, that is, how it contributes to the differential growth of the economy whose taxpayers sustain it (a growth designed to establish a widening of the gap between a wealthy nation and one less well-endowed). This, too, reduces ecology to economy. Yet surely there is substantially more to an ecology – to the university's worldliness – than its economy: there is more to the world and to the establishment of a social environment in which people live together than GDP, or than personal individual wealth.

It is here that we need to address the violence of a situation in which economics coerces ecology into silence. That ecology is better described in terms of the environment of the university itself, the civil society and its citizens who sustain it, authorize it and entitle it as a civil power: an authority.

1.5 THE SECULAR UNIVERSITY

Where, finally, should we stand in relation to the secular university? What is the relation of university to world in our times?

The days of the so-called 'ivory tower' are long gone, and it is unhistorical to want to make some kind of return there, to retreat from the world and worldliness. The university today is secular through and through. In this respect, it is entirely different from the monastic institutions and religious foundations that gave us the original 'idea of the university'. Our contemporary institutions are in and of the world, and this is a good thing.

However, it does not follow that the university should assume a position that accepts the world as it is. What follows is that the university's key questions and guiding principles are worldly, historical. Our preoccupations are and should be the world as a site of change and historical mutability. Rather than accepting 'what is the case', that Wittgensteinian version of 'the world' – Die Welt ist alles, was der Fall ist – we can construe the university instead as precisely the institution that cannot accept the world as what is the case. It is here that we imagine worlds undreamt of, and it is thus here that we imagine and then realize futures or simply historical and secular change. This to say: it is here that we can research and it is here that we can learn and teach. Crucial to both is the realization that one central thing that the university stands for is making history, not money.

We are of the world in that we assume a position among the forces that shape our social, cultural, political and economic constellations. This means that we should not be 'reacting' to the world as it is but should instead assume a proper responsibility to help shape it. This is our 'contribution' to the economy, to the politics, to the social and the personal: the realm of possibility.

For, in fact, we might say that, in the university, the world is everything that is not yet the case. We must acknowledge our place in the regime of forces. This means that we must act or become agents of possible futures and history. Along with the demise of the ivory tower, we also face the demise of the so-called 'disinterested' scholar. While maintaining a sceptical attitude that accepts empirical evidences for our researches, we should also acknowledge that our researches are necessarily 'directed'. There are things that the university does, spontaneously.

'What are Universities for?' asked Stefan Collini. We might also ask 'What are Universities against?' Collini's question presupposes a kind of neutral answer, investigating what it is that universities do to serve the social domain that subtends them. But we can also hear 'for' in terms of what is it that our current system supports and subtends: are we 'for' scientific progress; are we 'for' aesthetic beauty; are we 'for' the amelioration of social conditions? And so on. We might answer these all in the affirmative. However, that is itself a purely ideal picture. In empirical fact, and by contrast, the university as currently constituted is above all 'for' inequality. It should be against it.

At stake, then, is our university ecology: how do we speak of or how do we describe our place in the world? This question is indeed of global significance. In the 20th century, the post-Second World War world united in what became a successful attempt to eliminate smallpox. The progress here required political will and cooperation among nations for the public good. None of this was for private advantage or competition. Today, we face a similar worldwide problem that, like smallpox, threatens the future of life itself. The university's priorities should be clear in this context. We need to face the force of nature; we need to address how our own forces of circumstance – the way we live now, as Trollope once put it – is affecting and afflicting the natural environmental realm. Like those GIs who came to the US institutions after 1945, we are caught between the priority of the life of the mind and the very survival of the body. We need to face the force of nature when it comes in the form of all kinds of bullying behaviour, be that in direct physical wars or in indirect forms, as in economic warfare and structural inequality.

Now, more than ever, the university has to be worldly, to find ways of regulating the forces of nature and of circumstance that unite us, not in some 'global race' as the UK Prime Minister David Cameron puts it, not in some competition for advancement that will damn others to the place of losers, but rather forces that unite us in the realization of how some human activities jeopardize the life-chances of the next generation.

We owe a debt – to the world, and to the future generations, and it is to this that I turn in the next chapter.

2
DEBTS AND DUTIES OR OF TIME AND TRUST IN THE UNIVERSITY

> Politics is the alternative to chance and necessity.
>
> (Roberto Mangabeira Unger, *Democracy Realized*, Verso, 1998, p. 15)

2.1 ON ETHICS AS DUTY

For literary scholars and historians, it is well known that, in considering what she called 'the three words which have been used so often as the inspiring trumpet-calls of men' – the words God, Immortality and Duty – George Eliot 'pronounced, with terrible earnestness, how inconceivable was the *first*, how unbelievable the *second* and yet how peremptory and absolute the *third*'.[1] The duties to which ethics calls us do not depend on other-worldliness or on a religious threat in which we might find damnation – 'disagreeable consequences from the criminal laws of another world' as she put it in 'Worldliness and Other-worldliness'. Rather, for George Eliot, the duty that constitutes ethics is a peremptory demand, and we are called to it as a condition of our being human and of being together in the formation of societies.

In some ways, she prefigures a much more theologically committed thinker of a later century, Levinas. Both felt the ethical demand as a kind of 'duty', and a duty that followed simply from the fact of the necessity of our worldly being-together, of the simple fact that we live face-to-face with each other and not in atomized individuation and seclusion. In his recent study, *Together*, Richard Sennett proposes a distinction between ways of being-together in the world. He distinguishes 'sympathy' from 'empathy', arguing that 'Sympathy overcomes differences through imaginative acts of identification' (p. 21), and,

---

[1] Frederic W.H. Myers, 'George Eliot', *The Century Magazine* (November 1881).

in this, we establish a deep intimacy such that self and other 'forge a bond' that is like 'an embrace'. By contrast, 'empathy attends to another person on his or her own terms', and here the bond is closer to 'an encounter' (p. 21). This helps clarify the nature of a secular *collegium* as the site not of neo-Platonic embraces but of historical encounters grounded in an empathetic respect for difference and for others.

I will explore how the idea of an ethical duty pertains to the strength of a worldly university as the site where we encounter difference through empathetic engagement. In doing so, I shall explore the relation of duty to debt, specifically the debt that we owe to others. The articulation of that argument depends on an understanding not only of the relations between financial capital and intellectual capital, but also of the relation of capital as such to time: our debts to the past that forms us and to the future for which we must ethically assume some responsibility.

Indeed, the very word 'due', indicative not just of a temporality but also of something that is 'owed', derives from the same etymological root as debt itself: duty and debt are both marked by being 'dues', and in that word we find the first glimpse of what I take as the proper relation between capital and time. The idea of 'paying your dues' is a well-worn routine of blues music, and when B.B. King, for a classic example, sings 'Why I play the blues', with its chorus line of 'I've really, really paid my dues', he sings not only of the cultural and political history of the legacy of slavery, but also of a personal history, in which his relations to the contemporary world are laid out. The song lays out serial injustices – injustices related directly to the world of capital – across that time, and it exemplifies how we might see the relations between debt and justice, between 'paying your dues' and how that relates to social, cultural and political issues of secular injustice. At stake is the question of how we respond to injustice, as a matter of social duty.

If, as I maintain, the university is or should be a secular institution, then it follows axiomatically that we need to understand its relation to temporality. This runs all the way from the length of time it might take to complete a course of study for a degree, to the ways in which we structure or organize that time, to the issue of time–money 'efficiencies', to our relations with history and traditions and all the way on to the relation of our 'investments' in time and the debts that they incur. Central to this is an encounter whose ethical duty consists in a demand to transform the self. In an institution that is secular and worldly, the together-nature of the collegium must axiomatically engender change.

The university can be well characterized as 'an encounter that generates time' or that generates an openness to future possibility, an openness to difference and to change, for the world and our engagements with and in it.

'You must change your life', wrote Rilke, famously, and, in some ways, that is the foundational ground of a secular education. I want to explore this demand for the openness to change in terms of debts and duties.

2.2 OUR INTERGENERATIONAL DUTIES OR 'DEBT'

In her essay on 'Worldliness and other-worldliness', George Eliot launched a ferocious critical attack on Edward Young, author of 'Night Thoughts'. Her criticism combined personal diatribe (she saw Young as an individual of dubious propriety) with formal analysis (she saw the failure of his poem to engage authentic emotion as a consequence of his failure to attend to particularity and to adhere instead to forms of abstraction that would preclude empathy). The critique yields a finely nuanced and serious position that is central to our emerging concerns here.

Eliot argues that Young fails throughout his poem to attend to historical and material particularity. 'The adherence to abstractions ... is closely allied to the *want of genuine emotion*'. We never find Young considering things in the world as they really exist; so virtue or religion remain as abstract things, not as living tangible particularity. The result is inauthenticity and a failure to engage a reader who is not already of Young's persuasions, especially his religious persuasions. In short, Young talks to himself, with no dues or debts to others, and the result is that he looks not for dialogue with his reader but simple conformity to a pre-existing religious myth.

This inauthenticity, argues Eliot, is a fundamental structural failure in Young's entire ideological framework, his entire sensibility. Young believes that human virtue derives from a specific other-worldliness, in which any sense that we might have of justice derives not from historical particularity but from religiously inspired duty, from a fear that our duties/debts are being judged as from a world other than our own, a heavenly realm. In reply, Eliot imagines a response that says,

> I am just and honest, not because I expect to live in another world, but because, having felt the pain of injustice and dishonesty toward myself, I have a fellow-feeling with other men, who would suffer the same pain if I were unjust or dishonest toward them.

Our social being elicits the possibility of what Eliot calls sympathy and imagination (she does not make the nuanced distinction made by Sennett). Thus, 'Through my union and fellowship with the men and women I *have* seen, I feel a like, though a fainter, sympathy with those I have *not* seen'. This leads to the key aspect here that is of crucial relevance to the present argument. With such imaginative sympathy, writes Eliot, 'I am able so to live in imagination with the generations to come, that their good is not alien to me, and is a stimulus to me to labour for ends which may not benefit myself, but will benefit them'.

There is here an ethical duty or a debt towards the future, and explicitly towards future generations. This debt relates to what we would now call intergenerational justice, an issue that has become so pressing in recent times that the United Kingdom now hosts a think tank called the Intergenerational Foundation (see www.if.org.uk). One of their key epigrams is the celebrated quotation taken from Thomas Jefferson's letter to John Taylor on 28 May 1816: 'I sincerely believe ... that the principle of spending money to be paid by posterity under the name of funding is but swindling futurity on a grand scale'. Further, the debt in question – our 'dues' or the debt we owe to the future – is shaped by Sennett's 'empathy'.

A serious argument here will need to establish the relations, therefore, between time (that future-orientation), money (and its relation to debt and/or duty) and community (the nature of social empathy). If we can establish these relations properly, we will go some way towards understanding the relation of the university not only to time and to material history, but also to finance, to justice and to the public good. That public, importantly, consists of people other than ourselves, Eliot's 'men and women ... [whom] I have not seen'.

A duty and debt towards the future should be set in contrast with what, according to Eliot, Edward Young saw as the main thrust of religion. It is important to remember here that Eliot has already characterized Young as a man who has an eye on the main chance in terms of making an easy financial living; for him, she says, religion is properly characterized, in his own words, as '"ambition, pleasure, and the love of gain", directed towards the joys of the future life instead of the present'. In this, the 'future life' attended to is the individual's own life, seen as separate from a shared humanity in the material present world; but for Eliot, it is the future generations of other people, people whom I do not see but whom I can imagine as other than myself yet related to me, that matters. The debt or duty is general precisely because it is shaped by secularity and by worldliness: by the ethical condition of being-together that constitutes the question of justice and of 'just living'.

There are, then, at least two ways in which our 'virtue' – and, by extension in our present terms, the moral value of the university – can be directed towards the future. For Young, for whom religion operates much like capital investment, our eye is on the final prize for ourselves, in some world other than the material and historical world in which we live. For Eliot, by contrast, an ethics here is necessarily based upon an essential alterity – a feeling that is aware of the self's difference from others, but a difference of which we are conscious through an encounter that brings the self and other into proximity and engagement: duty.

Such an ethical stance stresses our debt towards future generations. In short, we might say that George Eliot pits 'Young' against 'the young' and weighs heavily towards the latter. The question is vibrant for us, today, because the prevailing view of the university, as described by governments in both developed and developing economies, is firmly oriented in favour of the former view – Young's thoroughly self-centred, individualistic, and literally 'selfish' view – that makes for a coalescing of religion and capital gain. The university is increasingly being driven, primarily by government policies, towards the service of individual 'ambition, pleasure, and the desire for gain', the only qualifications being that such gains are not just personal but also dependent upon personal and individual structures of financial debt. In some cases – the crudest versions being in televangelism, but equally apparent in much contemporary politics – this coalescing of religion and capital gain has now acquired the status of precisely the kind of fundamentalism that I criticized extensively in my opening chapter.

2.3 DEBTS BETWEEN PAST AND FUTURE

It is often asserted, however, that the university has a specific relation not to the future at all but rather to the past. A number of recent studies of what seems to be a crisis in higher education worldwide lay an emphasis on this. For Martha Nussbaum, in a consideration of US and also Indian institutions, 'the cultivation of imagination ... is closely linked to the Socratic capacity for criticism of dead or inadequate traditions'.[2] Andrew Delbanco, for another typical example, takes it as a fundamental principle 'that in order to comprehend problems of the present, it is helpful to know something about the past'.[3] He takes it that a key priority of higher education is cultivation of 'a sceptical discontent with the present, informed by a sense of the past' (p. 3). For him, teaching, 'at its best' is a 'generative act, one of the ways by which human beings try to cheat death – by giving witness to the next generation so that what we have learned in our own lives won't die with us' (p. 11).

In these examples, we get a sense of the university as an institution that gathers the past to itself, but it does so in order to mediate that past and the present, either through criticism that demands that we address the inadequacies of the past for our current predicaments (Nussbaum) or in order that we simply know more and try to 'cheat death' in a constant projecting of generations for future learning (Delbanco). Stefan Collini would add to this a fuller sense of the university as a median space, a mediating space between past and future.

In her essay collection, *Between Past and Future*, Hannah Arendt situates the identity of the human subject precisely in what she calls the 'gap' between past and future. Both past and future, she writes, exert a force on the human being,

---

[2] Martha Nussbaum, *Not for Profit* (Princeton University Press, 2010), 109.

[3] Andrew Delbanco, *College* (Princeton University Press, 2009), xiii.

and, indeed, the human is *identified* precisely by that clash of two opposing forces. However, in that tension (*die Spannung*) or 'gap', the subject herself or himself also exerts a force, and this force, 'whose origin is unknown, whose direction is determined by past and future, but whose eventual end lies in infinity, is the perfect metaphor for the activity of thought'.[4] Further, this 'gap' is identified as the site of a 'challenge' for the subject conditioned by it. In accepting the challenge – which is a challenge to act or initiate, using one's force as a way of regulating the competing demands of past and future – human beings 'create that public space between themselves where freedom could appear' (p. 4).

This 'mediating' force, between past and future, is itself identical with the university as such, for it is a location of 'the activity of thought', and, as such, it asks us to think in a manner that will allow freedom to appear. That which is 'free' is that which is not conditioned by 'debt' or by one's dues, and it is thus related directly to justice. The logic is simple: universities, properly constituted as a force between past and future, are generative of freedom and justice, provided they assert their proper historical identity.

For Collini, universities have become 'an important medium – perhaps the single most important institutional medium – for conserving, understanding, extending, and handing on to subsequent generations the intellectual, scientific, and artistic heritage of mankind'.[5] Collini and Delbanco, both writing from an English-literary disciplinary background, would know this kind of formulation regarding the medium and mediation most intimately from a great modernist essay, T.S. Eliot's 'Tradition and the Individual Talent', originally published in 1919 in *The Egoist*, some six months after Valéry's letters (discussed in Chapter 1) on the *Crisis of the Spirit* that appeared in the *Athenaeum*, a journal with which T.S. Eliot himself had close ties.

This celebrated essay poses an argument that is relevant to our consideration of time and tradition in relation to the university. The central plank of the argument is that tradition is not easily 'inherited'. Indeed, at one level, the essay can be read as a countervailing force against what was emerging at the time as a profoundly conservative, even reactionary, social thinking based upon precisely the same eugenics as we see being tentatively revived in the present day. Rather, the essay holds that one has to work at acquiring a tradition, and the acquisition involves a deep engagement with the past. It thereby sets the power of inherited wealth against the authority of autonomous labour. However, that engagement with the past, if genuine, enables the 'individual talent' to emerge, and the individual talent is she or he who, in their present

---

[4] Hannah Arendt, *Between Past and Future* (Penguin, London, 2006), 12.

[5] Stefan Collini, *What are Universities For?* (Penguin, London, 2012), 198.

moment and in the elaboration of their work, transforms the past. This is what makes the individual a 'modern', shaping history but not without reference to her or his own historical formation.

The past is re-formed, its intrinsic sense being re-shaped precisely by the individual talent who, in the new work, mediates the tradition *by transforming it*. Dialectically, the individual talent reveals herself as an individual talent precisely to the extent that she shows her *immersion in* the tradition by her *transformation of* the tradition. The new writer is herself now therefore an essential constituent element in the tradition, and not standing in discrete judgement or appreciation or even knowledge of it. The tradition – the past – is not something that stands aloof or disengaged as a series of static monuments: to know the tradition is already to have transformed it and to be transformed by it. What we call 'the present moment' is precisely the site of that transformation of the past into open possibilities for the future: *Spannung*. In the university seminar room, library or laboratory, it is called 'teaching' or 'learning' or, more commonly, both simultaneously.

This is one of many reasons why any contemporary talk of a university education that speaks of 'delivering' education or that talks of a university's 'offer' to students is inappropriate, wrong-headed and fundamentally anathema not only to education but also to human freedom, to secularity and to the intergenerational duty that we owe to the future. This mode of presentation of a university education reduces the past to a static series of monuments that can be 'bought', 'invested in' or 'inherited' like some other commodities within wealthy families. In trying to treat education in such mercantile business terms, it commits the error signalled in 1919 by Valéry. The reduction of education to a 'deliverable' commodity presented as a commercial 'offer' simply helps reassert inequalities based upon the 'sovereignty of nature' or upon the primacy of force, including the force of unequal and inherited wealth (what might be called a 'something-for-nothing' culture).

After all, as we know at least since Walter Benjamin, history and 'the past' are typically written by the victors, by those whose physical or 'natural' force allowed them to triumph over all others, living to tell the tale of the struggle but in their own self-privileging terms. To treat the past as a static commodity is thus to ignore the barbarism that lurks occluded within every document of 'civilization', as he put it in his seventh thesis on the philosophy of history: 'There is no document of civilization which is not at the same time a document of barbarism. And just as such a document is not free of barbarism, barbarism taints also the manner in which it was transmitted from one owner to another'.[6]

---

[6] Walter Benjamin, *Illuminations* (trans. Harry Zohn; ed. Hannah Arendt, Fontana, 1973), 258.

The uncritical mode of education – as an activity that 'delivers' the past tradition and simply 'hands it down' – belongs with Young and the ambitious pursuit of personal gain for one's own pleasure, regardless of the realities of our historical and material present world. Those who *believe* this language (as opposed to those who merely speak it) are engaged in a fundamental *trahison des clercs*; those who merely *speak* the language need to become aware of its consequences for establishing unquestioned but misguided norms for the sector and its students. It is the future generation's freedom to act and the possibility of extending both freedom and justice that are at stake.

The increasing normativity of education as a commodity or, in the jargon, as a 'deliverable offer' of compartmentalized 'modules' (like an IKEA flat-pack multi-form piece of furniture) assumes the false idea of the past as a settled and static tradition. In this view, tradition consists in and can be 'contained' in static elements, self-contained and carefully delimited modules that are like 'monuments of unageing intellect' (to misappropriate a phrase from Yeats's 'Sailing to Byzantium'). It is this kind of thinking that lay behind earlier debates about the humanities, such as we find them in the so-called 'theory wars' of the 1980s and 1990s. Conservatives such as Allan Bloom, Dinesh D'Souza and E.D. Hirsch defend 'the Great Books'; but they do so in the belief that these have a kind of consensually agreed value as 'the tradition'. Such books – and who chose them, and why? – are to stand as our uncritically assumed 'inheritance'. However, for T.S. Eliot (hardly a leftist revolutionary), tradition is very definitely not a matter of simple heritage, but rather something to be laboured over and struggled with. Reading and writing become an *agon*, as Harold Bloom will later call it: struggling for survival of the self (in Bloom's case, a psychic self) with and against the legacies of one's ancestors.

To teach these 'great books' as static monuments of greatness is not an education at all. Rather, it is, paradoxically, precisely that closing of the American mind – and of every mind – that Bloom ascribed to his 'theoretical' enemies. It proceeds as if the student is nothing but the passive recipient of the great thoughts. Her task is to internalize the values of 'the tradition', and, in this way, she is ready to assume her social role as one who will uphold that tradition as if it were unquestioningly normative. That is not education, but ideological conformism that stifles intellectual labour, requiring only docile assent with the pre-established values and norms that Bloom, D'Souza, Hirsch and other conservatives hold. Education, by complete contrast, adopts the position more like that of both George Eliot and T.S. Eliot: it sees that tradition has to be transformed if we are to enter the future as anything other than servile human resource or exchangeable human capital. The student is she or he who mediates in this transformative way; the active student occupies the 'moment' (in the sense taken from physics), described by Arendt, between past and future. The Prussians called it *Bildung*.

The significance of these arguments extends well beyond the so-called 'theory wars', beyond the walls of the classroom or laboratory. The subscription to some belief that we can regard the meanings of the great texts, say, as somehow 'settled', and as receptacles or vehicles of settled and agreed value, amounts to an attempt, essentially, to control the commemorations of the past itself. This has its clear political counterpart – and it is an unpleasant one. As Tzvetan Todorov has argued, 'The totalitarian regimes of the twentieth century sought to achieve total control of memory. Such a dangerous ambition had never been thought of before'.[7] This – totalitarianism – ghosts some of the restrictive conservative practices that are increasingly the neo-liberal and managerial norm in our institutions.

Todorov points out that the means to achieve this total control of memory are various. They start with the elimination of evidence – which we, today, might consider in terms of the censorship in various ways of dissident or 'unnatural' (that is, unconventional) voices. One example would be the once woman-free zone of the English literary curriculum. A second technique, he says, is 'to *intimidate* people and to forbid them to seek information or to pass it on' (p. 114), and again, we today would see this in the demand for conformity with the university's corporate brand, the demand to be always 'on-message' with the corporate line, and the intimidation – through techniques such as isolation via suspensions and the like – of staff who again dare to think, much less express, dissident views. The third means, argues Todorov, is through euphemism (Klemperer's 'language of the third Reich', Orwell's 'Newspeak'). He gives examples such as 'final solution', 'special treatment', 'transportation', 'evacuation' and the like. It is no great stretch from this to the current prevalence of 'managementese' – the whole gamut of managerialist jargon and linguistic vacuities and obfuscating subterfuge – that scars the language in which and by which the academic community is controlled.

That language – managementese – is precisely the marker of an incipiently totalitarian cult. Liz Morrish has exposed astutely how it operates. She shows how there is, in the academy, a conflict between academic priorities and the language in which managerialism tries to encompass those values. It is a story of how management co-opts the academic, as the language 'works by forcing the academic to cite discourse which redefines their subjectivity in terms of managerial values'. Further, given the utter vacuity of the language, Morrish gives a brilliant analogy to explain how the cult works: it is like a

---

[7] Tzvetan Todorov, *Hope and Memory* (trans. David Bellos; Atlantic Books, London, 2005), 113.

Ponzi scheme. Such schemes 'endow investors with riches, not on the basis of enhancing productivity; instead the flow of money is only guaranteed when you can persuade new investors to join the scheme'.[8] Many an academic has succumbed to these Ponzi schemes, and most know that the basis of their leadership authority is fragile. Hence we get not authority but over-stated authoritarianism instead of engagement in reasoned argument or democratic debate.

Summing this kind of situation up in a wider political and historical context, Todorov writes that 'Free access to the past *unfettered by centralized control* [stress here added] is one of the fundamental, inalienable freedoms of democratic countries, alongside freedom of expression and freedom of thought' (p. 118). The passage that I have stressed here is crucial: the conservative attitude to education as a commodity requires that the past be 'controlled' by a central power that we call 'authority' or 'established value', such that the past remain unchanged, unchanging and immovable. Academic work – *thinking* – must be 'managed' and not 'represented', and thereby controlled.

The democratic task is not to 're-write the past' in the manner of those totalitarian regimes that purge now-disgraced or out-of-favour politicians, say, photoshopping them out of the historical record, but the task is one where the *meanings* of the past must remain open to ongoing dialogue and debate, especially in the light of fresh and new thinking or information. In this way, the past can indeed be reconsidered, in precisely the ways that it was in the wake of revelations about the Nazi atrocities, say, when the meanings of 'the camps' underwent significant semantic change.

The political counterpart to this is equally well described by Roberto Mangabeira Unger as a form of 'democratic experimentalism'. It is not the case that the individuals act alone, nor is it the case that only institutions or society as an imagined whole can act meaningfully. The 'democratic experimentalist' subscribes to the view that individual emancipation can intersect with practical social progress and that the intersection of these two claims – often construed as rivals or even opposing forces – can be found in institutional conditions. Importantly, and axiomatically, this is also a function of education in the terms that I am describing it here. Here is Unger:

> Both practical progress and individual emancipation depend upon the capacity to transform social effort into collective learning ... undeterred by a need to respect a pre-established plan of social division and hierarchy or a confining

---

[8] Liz Morrish, 'Institutional discourse', available at: http://www.discoversociety.org/2014/05/06/institutional-discourse-and-the-culture-of-managerialism/

allocation of social roles. Such constraints are particularly subversive of collective discovery and invention when they reflect inherited advantage, for they then fall like a blind and irresistible fate upon all forms of individual striving.[9]

This formulation is useful in stressing 'collective' discovery or learning, the kind of learning that happens in the collegium of a seminar, say. Paradoxically, the conservative thesis is one that actually works to oppress the individual, forcing her or him to abandon the possibility of any individual or new insight, and to conform instead simply to those pre-established rules, which the conservative teacher calls 'the tradition'. Such a view not only denies individual talent, but also precludes the very possibility of a collegium or a community of learning and scholarship.

For the conservative, there is no need for a classroom or a laboratory: a purely transactional MOOC or 'Massive Online Open Course' – with atomized individuals who can be kept under technological surveillance by anonymous centralized and controlling virtual 'teachers' – will do the business, thereby also progressively eliminating not only the need for a teacher but also the possibility of an individual thought that might stretch beyond the regime of economic transaction or, as it is more usually called, 'shopping'. There is the world of difference between the 'virtual' teacher and the 'virtuous' teacher, and the latter is increasingly in danger of disappearing under the former, as shopping replaces the very idea of virtuous ethical engagement within the university. The supposed immediacy of transaction rids us of the time that we might need for thinking, studying or engaging with the events of the past and the possibilities of the future.

And what is the reason for this shopping? We find the answer in the mantra of personal gain, private advantage in a 'competitive' society. This ideology fundamentally constitutes an attack on the very being of 'the student', reducing her or him to the status of 'customer' and denying the possibility of an education. The customer, of course, is one who not only shops, but also who is governed by 'custom' or normative habit, and 'customs' are also, of course, a tax on imported goods, implying and enforcing centralized and governmental control on otherwise free exchange. Education reduced to shopping is profoundly immoral, unethical – and, in recent times, especially in the United Kingdom, designed to drive the young into personal debt as a means of preserving the inherited wealth of those whose authoritative position in the world is already established.

Christopher Newfield, in his *Unmaking the Public University* (Harvard, 2008), revealed what is at stake in this conservative culture, specifically in the US

---

[9] Roberto Mangabeira Unger, *Democracy Realized* (Verso, London, 1998), 6–7.

context. He showed how the so-called 'theory wars' in the United States were not, as is usually thought, wars that were launched by colleagues engaged in 'theory' and continental strains of philosophy. Rather, the theory wars were actually wars declared on the humanities by conservative ideologues who feared the democratizing influence that this kind of proper and open education can have. These conservative cultural warriors offered – in the guise of a supposed openness – a real reduction of the spirit. Their education represented a narrowing of possibility. In fact, it was precisely a recipe for the *failure* to engage with the tradition, while at the same time an *appropriation* of it in the form of 'inherited' intellectual capital, and this intellectual capital, of course, is instrumental also in the enhancing of financial capital.

For those who share this conservative view of tradition, and of the university's position with regard to time and to history, there is no such thing as a collegium. We are not students but rather functionaries and operatives of a system that is essentially and fundamentally driven by the demands of both GDP growth and the preservation of individual (especially inherited) wealth. It is important that we reduce the expansive possibilities for transformation that are offered by knowledge, into the slimmer and more repetitive but narrowed functions of 'skills'. Finally, it is also important that access to this inherited wealth be retained as exclusive and authorized by governmental control: it is another version of an act of enclosure of the intellectual commons, but one that encloses time itself, as well as or alongside earlier enclosures of space, land or territories, and, like them, it is grounded in force – this time the force of inherited and unearned financial wealth: the unearned authority that we call privilege.

2.4 FROM DUTY AND DEBT TO DISCIPLINE AND PUNISH

What would the opposite be? What might it mean positively to engage tradition as a transformative experience, to make our engagement with the past into a transformative encounter that acknowledges our historical being-together in a world whose future is at stake? It would mean taking our time (in every sense) and also in making our time (making the future something that is open to new possibility), and it would entail taking seriously an idea of contested progress and an orientation of our duty and debt to future generations. There is, as it were, an intergenerational contract in any society that recognizes the possibility and even the need for historical change, for making and remaking a shared world. In the standard classic teaching situation, of course, such a responsibility to future generations is, quite si   mply, a reassertion of a responsibility to our students, *as students* and not as 'customers', 'clients', 'consumers', 'purchasers of our services', 'future human capital', 'potential workforce' and so on.

It is a shocking indictment of how far gone we are on the knowledge-is-commerce road that such a simple statement needs to be rehearsed at the present time. Let me say it again: *we are students; we are not human capital; we are not human resources*. More often, and in contrast with this truth, teaching faculty and staff are reminded of their institutional accountabilities, including demands or expectations to boost all sorts of income, to boost the institutional brand, to avoid any statement that might be construed as criticism in case it jeopardizes brand-reputation, to file patents, to carry the brand logo on correspondence, to encourage the purchase of branded merchandise and so on.[10]

With this shift in priorities, there has been a concomitant shift in the question of our academic duties. The logic was simple at first, but it has now yielded a significant contradiction. At first, there was a translation of the question of our sociocultural duties into a different kind of debt: given that universities were largely funded by the general taxpayer, the logic was taken to imply that we as academics had a primary duty to serve our paymasters. The paymasters, in daily terms, were the institutions themselves, as quasi-autonomous self-governing bodies. Thus, it follows that our duty is to our senior managers: in a word, to the institution itself and its metonymic manifestation in the figure of the VC, whose own position becomes one of super-manager. Many VCs have embraced this. However, if the logic of my case is right, essentially those who do so are embracing what looks like an authoritative position but is only an authoritarian one: a degradation that makes them as effective in the world of historical realities as the parody figure of the Fat Controller in the series of *Thomas the Tank Engine* books for children.

Thus it was that our duty to students was replaced by a required allegiance to our institutional leaderships, those who determine the brand and keep the academy running and in line, literally, through systems of managerial 'line-management', a management style that brooks no opposition or debate. We have here an interesting confrontation of two modes of pedagogical philosophy. On one hand, we have a Socratic mode of quizzical questioning, which involves dialogue and debate. This can be associated with the emergence of a specific kind of democracy, as the pursuit of the best argument through the operation of reasoned logic and shared understandings. On the other hand, we have a reverence for past learning, resembling the attitude of Confucius to the great masters of the past. There is a choice here, and it is not simply a pedagogical choice, but a political one.

---

[10] For a good illustration of how all this works, see Mariana Mazzucato, *The Entrepreneurial State* (Demos, 2011), 50–52, on patents and the Bayh-Dole Act of 1980; available at: http://www.demos.co.uk/files/Entrepreneurial_State_-_web.pdf.

It is my contention here that students, insofar as they are students at all, are people who debate. There follows a strained tension in terms of where our duties lie. The universities of the so-called advanced or 'western' economies and their leadership resolved this tension through the establishment of monitoring and auditing systems – often going well beyond any form of legal or statutory requirements – whose purpose is to determine academic *behaviour*. That behaviour had to be consistent with whatever the university management decided as its key priorities; but those priorities themselves were coming under further strain. Confucius wrestles with Socrates, as it were.

The leadership of the sector, seemingly terrified of ever saying 'No' to governments of whatever colour, fell into line and step with the general ideological tendency of the last half a century: a drift towards what the political class insisted on calling 'modernization' (another Ponzi term), and that Helena Kennedy calls 'The London orthodoxy', according to which it is taken for granted that 'markets should drive social and economic development, that competition is the primary motor for that development and that the role of the state is to give the market its head'.[11] Thus, the universities become hostages to that kind of coercive 'public opinion' that has monetized all values, and the logic of this is the outsourcing, to the market, of all duties, now reconfigured in terms of private debt.

Outsourcing has become a major lever of the fundamental commercialization of knowledge in the university, and thus also a major determinant of the immorality that attacks the student-as-student, replacing her with the student-as-consumer who is indebted *financially* but not *ethically*.

For a simple example, outsourcing of food outlets on campus is designed to establish brand loyalty among faculty and students for specific high-street enterprises who pay the necessary franchise to advertise their high-street operations via campus 'consumer capture' and so on. More generally, outsourcing of services, including security services, is driven either by the demand to reduce wages for ancillary staff or, in extreme forms, to convert the very nature of the campus. Instead of the campus being a shared space for the exploration of knowledge, it becomes like a 'private' property in the ownership of senior management, who increasingly routinely call on the police or other outsourced security services to quash any action, voice or thought that might dissent from the preferred values of its 'owner'. As I noted in the earlier chapter – and as is now well detailed in video and YouTube footage – the presence of 'cops on campus' is not only intimidating but also a clear manifestation of how the university authorities, having lost reasoned argument or debate, turn, in the final instance, to violence against students or to bogus disciplinary actions against staff.

---

[11] Helena Kennedy, 'No divorce', *New Statesman* (28 February 2014), 31

Such actions are entirely in line with the 'disciplining' of academics and their behaviour, to ensure that they are acknowledging their dutiful service to senior management, rather than to their students, their departments and their academic disciplines themselves. This gives a menacing substance to the Ponzi scheme underlying the managerialist ascendancy, and it eradicates ethics from our collegial duty. Private sector modes of 'Human Resource' management are inappropriately incorporated into the sector, and these will include that form of censorship known as 'suspension' from duties. Many institutions have provision for statutory suspension of academic colleagues, usually pending investigations of alleged wrongdoing.

However, 'wrongdoing' now extends to cover anything that can be classed as dissent – including what was once regarded as a proper professional *duty* to debate, argue or criticize. Instead of students and academics having an egalitarian collegiality and affiliation, managerialism and HR officers now require that we abandon such 'horizontal' affiliations with each other and replace them with 'vertical' affiliations to the hierarchy of leadership. In effect, this is designed to ensure that we have a 'duty-to-obey', and it is a one-way duty in that those lower down the authoritarian chain have to obey those above them, while those above can continue to exert power without fear of open recrimination or criticism. Criticism is now a punishable offence.

Institutionally, the disciplinary modes that eventuate in suspension – preliminary to termination of employment – operate at a level of abstraction that pretends to be neutral. Indeed suspension itself is regarded as a 'neutral act' and not prejudicial to the career or personal health of the suspended colleague. This may well be the case in private sector or commercial activity. There is, however, an interesting legal case that calls this mode of governance in professional institutions such as the university into question. The case of *Mezey vs Southwest London and St George Mental Health NHS Trust, 2007* finds that:

> at least in relation to the employment of a qualified professional in a function which is as much a vocation as a job, suspension changes the status quo from work to no work, and it inevitably casts a shadow over the employee's competence. Of course this does not mean that it cannot be done, but it is not a neutral act.[12]

> Case No: A2/2007/0062

---

[12] See http://www.bailii.org/ew/cases/EWHC/QB/2007/62.html and cf. Neutral Citation Number [2007] EWCA Civ 106; see http://www.bailii.org/ew/cases/EWCA/Civ/2007/106.html. I am indebted to my lawyers, Emma-Christine O'Keefe and Katie Lancaster of Farrer & Co., as also to my barrister, Paul Greatorex of 11KBW, for this and other similar examples.

We can extrapolate from this. 'Line-management' modes of staff management are increasingly being established as normative; but they are so established in dubious circumstances, in that their establishment changes the nature of one's professional duties. They also require the elimination of memory (as in Todorov's analysis), and the consequence of this is the eradication of the authority that an academic might have as a result of her or his remembered experience in the job. In the cult of managerialism, one is only ever as good as one's last class, one's last article and one's last hour's work: constant surveillance and keeping people in line isolates their every living moment, depriving them of their professional duties, of their professional authority and even of their professional history. This is why HR offices no longer pay any attention to the *cv*, preferring instead the so-called 'competency assessment'.

In sum, under the current dispensation, students and faculty are enjoined to be docile and to regard the possibility of historical change – even in how we think, in 'changing our minds' – as unnatural and therefore intrinsically prohibited. There is to be no secularity, no history: tomorrow will be the same as today, and any 'change' will be a purely cosmetic effect designed to protect the wealth and riches inherited from the past.

Thus, instead of a university existing in order to question social, cultural and political inequalities, it will, perhaps, allow a small number of under-privileged individuals to gain access to such wealth. By 'widening participation', which often amounts to co-opting a very small number of under-privileged people into the university's neo-liberal project, the university claims to be 'just'. 'Look,' it says, 'can't you see that we admitted that student from his deeply impoverished background? If he can do it, anyone can'. And thus the university absolves itself of any proper social responsibility for a world of massive structural inequality, preferring instead to internalize a logic of aggressive competitiveness for individual gain and self-advancement.

Democracy – and its demands for togetherness, for empathy – is reduced in this way to liberalism in its crudest economistic and monetized form. The task of the teacher is not to teach or to study, but rather simply and crudely to produce good and active consumers, and to do so for short-term or immediate financial gain. Any attitude of respect for larger-scale history is regarded as irrelevant to the immediate needs – now reduced to merely financial and economic needs – of the society that the university is supposed to serve. Thinking is outlawed, but so also is *saying* that 'thinking is outlawed'. The ascent of managerialism has turned ethical duty inside out and replaced it with the managing of our place in unchanging hierarchy: power to whom truth cannot be spoken.

2.5 EFFICIENCY AND ITS DISCONTENTS: THE UZBEKISTAN PRINCIPLE

What is the proper cultural engagement with time, with tradition and with the past? Crucially, if it involves transformation, then it is an engagement whose boundaries cannot be contained or 'enclosed' and managed. The primary reason that it escapes containment is because it escapes static presence: it is an event, and an event that is characterized by transformation. That is to say: it takes time, and requires delay. We used to just call this 'study', in the sense that I might stand for hours, days or weeks even, before a single painting, say, studiously looking at it and experiencing not just it and its changing appearance but also studying how I myself changed and am changing through that encounter. Just as this happens with the study of a painting, so also, if we are 'students' and not operatives of the neo-liberal economy, it happens with any disciplinary field. Sometimes, of course, we have to look and study for quite a long time, as with the fifty-plus years that it took to confirm the existence of the Higgs Boson, say.

Time, however, is – like space in our collegia – at a premium, and the university no longer countenances the possibility of a free inquiry whose results – intellectual or financial – are not more or less *immediately* apparent and realizable. We do not have too much time for study. Outcomes of research – and its 'impact' – have to be predicted, and this represents a reduction of time to the extent that the research even appears to have been carried out, successfully, even before it is funded – and even as a condition of its being funded in the first place. Research is directed largely towards 'near-market' uses in the interests of short-term financial profit, which is the kind of impact that Research Councils really have in mind. The assessment of teaching has to be almost instantaneous, with results and feedback given to students within unreasonably short time spans, such that the examiner or teacher has no time to engage properly with the student's thinking.

All of this eradication of time is especially warranted if and only if we regard study – axiomatically, what students do – as simply a somewhat irritating activity that has to be undergone in our otherwise seamless passage into becoming human resource, into employment, consumption and economic activity measured by GDP growth. This attitude is one that is governed by what I will call 'the efficiency myth'. Robert and Edward Skidelsky point out that such a myth is predicated upon poverty: 'The perspective of poverty, and with it an emphasis on efficiency at all costs, is built into modern economics'.[13] In this, they are building on a Kantian idea of leisure as 'purposiveness without

---

[13] Robert Skidelsky and Edward Skidelsky, *How Much is Enough?* (Penguin, London, 2013), 12.

purpose', and from Bertrand Russell, from whose *In Praise of Idleness* they quote: 'There was formerly a capacity for light-heartedness and play which has been to some extent inhibited by the cult of efficiency' (p. 11).

The efficiency myth — in the form of a calculated 'opportunity cost' associated with the otherwise economically advantageous time that one gives over to learning or study — is partly responsible for the foreshortening of study time, and it combines with a more general notion of performative optimization that is increasingly central to university activities. At one level, performative optimization appears to be non-controversial: who would argue against 'optimizing' by 'performing' well? Who would argue against efficiency? Yet, the adoption of this as a norm *for study* as opposed to *for production of commodities* has adverse effects. Above all, it changes our attitude to time itself.

Time has a deep relation to trust. Consider the most basic financial transaction: shopping. At the core of this is an attitude to time. Capital activity establishes a state of affairs where the future conditions the present: I hand over my money *now*, at the present moment, on condition that the *then*, a future when you hand me a coat, say, is guaranteed by trust. That is to say, I act *as if* the future has already happened. There is, in this, a radical foreshortening of time itself. Stiglitz considers what happens with such a 'shorting', as we might call it after the 2008 financial crisis. In *The Price of Inequality*, he explores various conditions in which 'social capital', which he describes as 'the glue that holds societies together', is relatively strong or weak. Where it is strong, there is a good deal of trust, and cooperation leads to the strengthening of both economic and ethical activities for the common good. Where it is weak, where 'each family look[s] out for itself', we lose trust and social bonds. Stiglitz describes the situation in Uzbekistan just after the fall of the USSR, where

> Most greenhouses had no glass, making them ineffective ... The glass was stolen from the greenhouses. Nobody was sure what they would do with the stolen glass, but it provided some limited security, and they were sure that if they didn't steal it, somebody else would [14]

'Uzbekistan' is increasingly the norm, insofar as it shapes the intrinsic nature and structure of universities. In 1987, Margaret Thatcher famously said that there was no such thing as society, rather there were only individuals and their families. The radical atomization of the social in this statement covers precisely the isolationism that refuses trust as a social bond. The consequence, in due course, is that the university — like so much else — becomes seen as

---

[14] Joseph Stiglitz, *The Price of Inequality* (Penguin, London, 2013), 154.

purely a private good, governed by short-term calculation. This is now taken as so normative that it is increasingly difficult to get an audience for the view that such a public-funded system can be a social good precisely because it engenders the social bond of trust and, with that, also generates time as an open future that can be shaped by the next generation. Trust is threatened when small numbers of these families start to accumulate personal wealth or to privatize what was once commonly held and shared public goods. The 'stolen glass', like privatized social utilities, works as a means of arresting the possibility of change: these are a kind of assault upon time, upon the openness of the future, and they ensure that future societies face a lack of cohesion through the elimination of trust. The elimination of trust and the elimination of time go hand in hand.

The question behind this is one of political will. The argument against state-funded universities in England (not in the United Kingdom as a whole) goes like this: in the 1950s, when only 5% went to university, we could afford to pay for it out of general taxation. However, we now have a mass system, and it is therefore no longer possible or efficient to fund it in the same way. Therefore, individuals must pay, not society as a whole. There is a sleight of hand here. Universities were state-funded until 1997, when participation was around 39%. As I write, in 2014, participation is about 49%. That 10-percentage-point increase represents the low hundreds of thousands of students, each to be funded for three years. Compare that with the political will shown by Nye Bevan in 1948, when he opened the National Health Service. Then, in a period so austere that even food was rationed, we committed general funding from society as a whole, going from 0 to 100% health cover overnight, and this was for some 50 million people, and for life. Social duty, exemplified in this, has ceded place to individualized debt.

The acquisition of knowledge-as-commodity – rather like the fake degree certificates that people can buy and trade through disreputable institutions worldwide – is an attempt to avoid duty. Most especially, it is an attempt to avoid paying our dues towards the future and towards an unknown possibility in that future, whose mystery requires the establishment of trust, and trust, of course, requires togetherness. Yet we also need to be wary of a drift towards a kind of neo-futurism that might be thought to lie latent here. The next section here explores why we also need caution.

2.6 ON FINANCIAL AND EDUCATIONAL 'SHORTING'

On the morning of 20 February 1909, readers of *Le Figaro* in Paris were roused by a front-page article written by F.T. Marinetti: the *Futurist Manifesto*. Scorning past and established traditions, Futurists wanted tomorrow today, and the *Manifesto* was a document that, albeit indirectly, shaped a dominant idea of our contemporary university: the worship of 'a new beauty: the beauty of speed'. Universities are now driven by similar kinds of structural and structured impatience, usually masked as efficiency.

One pertinent manifestation of speed's ostensibly unquestionable desirability lies in Anant Agarwal's claims for the feedback mechanisms in his massive open online course platform, EdX. Agarwal is the President of EdX, the Harvard- and MIT-funded MOOC, and, in *The New York Times International Supplement* of 14 April 2013, he is reported to be producing 'instant-grading software'. Submit your essay or coursework online and as your finger leaves the 'send' button, the grade and response feedback is instantaneously in your mailbox. It is not only instantaneously graded and returned, but it is also returned with suggestions for improvement. Agarwal thinks this is good, a boost to efficiency, as it will 'free professors up for other tasks'; but it is worth exploring the logical consequences.

Let us look closely, therefore, at what this extraordinarily radical foreshortening of time means. Agarwal says that 'There is a huge value in learning with instant feedback'. Understandably, there is a popular demand for quick turnaround of submitted and assessed work. As soon as one closes an exam paper, one wants the result, because this is a test and one seeks confirmation of one's competence, validation or professional accreditation. It often has as much at stake as would be the case with a medical examination or a biopsy, say, to which, equally one wants the results quickly. However, in these latter cases, you certainly want the result to be based upon judgement. That is what is lacking in the instant-return software.

Certainly, the software will be extraordinarily sophisticated, based on very advanced artificial intelligence research. Yet it is necessarily automated, not autonomous. The automation depends upon a programme, and that programme is made by a programmer or team of programmers. The machine 'decides' as correct that which the programmers have themselves already decided as correct. In even the most sophisticated cases, this can only mean – in an automatic, as opposed to autonomous, machine – acting in conformity with prior expectation. In short, the correct answer is pre-programmed. Essays will be corrected and graded in accordance with how much conformity they show with respect to that norm. As for repeated submission: the 'better grade' secured simply means better-because-in-greater-conformity with what the machine has been programmed to expect as a norm.

Paradoxically, and no doubt unintentionally, this yields an inversion of software such as 'TurnItIn', which is designed to detect – and punish – plagiarism, on the grounds that plagiarized essays do not demonstrate autonomous learning or autonomous thought on the part of the guilty writer. Here, however, with software that promises 'improvement' with revision, it is as if plagiarism is *required*, in the shape of requiring a rewriting that will be in greater conformity with some idealized 'perfect' answer or norm. Ethical duty here is turned on its head.

Further, in this way, the shrinking of time leads to an emphasis being placed on the mechanical and automated nature of the assessment *process*, but the actual work is not judged or examined at all; rather it is simply made to conform to a prejudged model – or, in short, to *prejudice*, which is the very opposite of rational thinking. Institutionalized prejudice is also, surely, to be resisted in the name of ethical duty. The virtuous, again, is being trumped by the virtual, and the autonomous student is being trumped by the automaton. In criticizing and opposing such a situation, I am in line with Robert and Edward Skidelsky, when they try to 'revive the old idea of economics as a *moral* science; a science of human beings in communities, not of interacting robots' (p. 6). And, just as things should be in economics, so they should also be in the university: that is, we should be concerned with how humans live together, and not with robotic functions.

Further, the software is designed to deal with 'massive' open online courses, and the hint is in the name: it is dealing with a mass system, with high numbers of participants. The key is that it is trying to process large amounts of work with maximum output and minimum input. It is driven by efficiency, performativity and 'optimization' of the mechanical procedures. It is not driven by being-together, by commonly sharing in order to allow for study. The straightforward complaint from the academic community is that it gets rid of the teacher, but actually, it also gets rid of the student, for it gets rid of the entire process of study. It does this by the elimination of time, by the pretence that the results of study can be acquired through a radical condensing of time.

The appropriate parallel that helps us to understand this is found in the operations of capital, especially in stock exchanges worldwide. Since 2008, we have become more aware of how financial transactions are no longer carried out by human agents. Computers use algorithms to process data infinitely more quickly than human brains can: the computer, as if fulfilling a futurist dream (maybe just a 'futures' dream), brings tomorrow's decisions today. Those we used to call 'share owners' can now hold a company's shares for less than a microsecond. This has serious consequences.

In this state of affairs, the company in question is no longer functionally a company at all: it has become a mere shell, a vehicle through which transactions take place in order to generate wealth for individuals who have no commitment to, or even interest in, what the company actually does. The algorithm determines activity based solely on maximizing profit, regardless of the content or practices of the company or business in question.

Increasingly, however, the same thing happens with the university: governments divest themselves of state interest in our substantive activities, provided that we are useful vehicles – shell companies – for wealth creation. Who now sees our priorities as grounded in the intellectual work once integral to our institutional identity? Who cares about communities of knowing that are made possible by the university's existence? What do these things matter in the face of a machine for enriching individuals whose intellectual commitments to study have been deliberately reduced by policy that requires their accumulation of personal debt and who are thereby diverted into the prioritization of economic self-interest?

The logic of the MOOC, and its associated 'speed-efficiency opportunity-cost model' – which can be carried out also in non-electronic and non-virtual modes – is clear. The prioritization of speed yields an 'efficiency' whose effect is to evacuate the university of thought, and to transform it into an empty carcass, a shell designed to be a mere initiation rite through which one enters the hallowed realm of personal wealth acquisition. It is little wonder that such an institution might want to eliminate thought: who, reflecting on themselves and their activity in the university, would want actively and willingly to identify this as their task?

Well, some clearly do. Private and for-profit institutions, such as the University of Buckingham in the United Kingdom, aim to profit precisely from this model. Their explicitly 'opportunity-cost' model of the efficient degree machine lets them parade their shortened degree structure. Why invest three years when you can get a degree in two? 'Getting the degree' here, seen as a passport to wealth, supplants the idea of 'taking time to think'. Logically, then, why waste two years? Won't a MOOC allow you to get through all the procedures in about a fortnight of sustained clicking through some videos, themselves typically pretty short and speedy? No need to wait for engagement with a teacher for feedback: just press 'send' and then do as you are told when the screen yields the feedback.

This is the pedagogical equivalent of financial 'shorting'.

Buckingham claims to condense 'the academic content' of a standard three-year programme; but, in glossing this, it explains that such a condensation simply involves increasing contact time: 'By offering 36 teaching weeks per year, we can fit in the same amount of teaching in two years as other universities spread over three'. This is true, of course. However, it appears to assume that a degree consists in 'teaching'. So, logically, why stop there? Why not deliver all the lectures and seminars in one continuous loop, in which case the condensation could be reduced to about 350 hours, roughly a fortnight. Clearly ludicrous, one might say, for one would need to ask 'what about learning' or 'what about study'?

How does Buckingham – like any private and for-profit institution – make sense of this fast-track degree? The answer is: money and the acquisition of private gain. 'You can complete a degree and earn a year's salary in the time it would take you *to study* for the same undergraduate degree at a state-subsidised university' [emphasis added]. Thus, 'the overall cost of a degree here is competitive with other universities – and you have the chance to start earning a year earlier as well'.[15] We should note the actual wording: no doubt unintentionally, there is a clear distinction between 'completing' or 'getting' a degree in Buckingham and 'studying for a degree' at other universities.

This condensation of time eliminates the study – as it must do (so this is not simply an accident of wording). The relation to economic priorities is also made clear: a better economic return for a smaller financial outlay. The argument is that this is not an education, but an investment, and, crucially, it is a 'fast-track' investment: it reduces the time between outlay and return. Many of their academics 'have a background in business or industry and can offer networking opportunities for students' is the boast on the 'graduate employment' page of the website.

If such networking were seen as a way to ensure the securing of highly-paid employment in other jurisdictions, we would probably simply think of it as 'corruption'. It is exactly equivalent to the crisis in democracy that is outlined by Stiglitz in his examination of the lobbying industry in US government, through which the richest manage to pervert legislation to work in their own favour and for the furthering of their private wealth. It is also entirely consistent with the workings of the financial sector of worldwide stock exchanges, where 'shareholders' may not even know that they are holding shares in particular companies: their 'interest' is not in any concrete business, but simply in using business for the private acquisition of money.

That model – based on the worship of speed, of money and of a bogus efficiency mistaken as 'throughput' – diminishes the university and demeans the student. Feedback, after all, is not just a one-way delivery statement: it is an extension of work done through discussion, which takes time. Anything else is just an invoice, the bureaucratic processing of students as fodder for a system corrupted by a wicked immorality that reduces thought to mere commodities for sale. In 1914, Futurists argued that thought itself is a commodity and that

---

[15] Quotations here are taken from Buckingham website, accessed 24 April 2014. See http://www.buckingham.ac.uk and http://www.buckingham.ac.uk/about/twoyear.

its price can be quantified by measurement. This – which seemed outrageous at the time the Futurists proposed it – has now been fully realized in the audit culture that governs virtually all activity in university institutions.

A chilling endorsement of speed comes from Daphne Koller, one of Coursera's MOOC founders: with instant feedback, she says, 'learning turns into a game, with students naturally gravitating toward resubmitting the work until they get it right'. In this context, 'getting it right' means 'conforming' to the expectations generated by algorithms. 'Excellence' means knowing one's place, obediently playing the game whose rules are made by others, conforming to what they call 'correct'. This is not education, rather it is the policing of behaviour, and it reduces the time for thought or communal engagement. It is another way of having cops-on-campus.

The real enemy of speedy efficiency is democracy itself. Amartya Sen follows J.S. Mill in describing democracy as 'government by discussion'. Discussion requires not just those ethical duties required by being-together in the world, but also that we slow down enough to listen to others and to think, patiently, with a view to making tomorrow a tomorrow and thus different from today. If we are genuinely interested in learning and in universities, we should argue for a further investment of time – longer degrees – to allow communities to 'govern by discussion'.

Marinetti's Futurism advocated the destruction of libraries and ended up standing alongside Mussolini. Our universities are in danger of catching up with that discredited past. In the end, the speed-efficiency model also entails the destruction of the university itself. Indeed, Sebastian Thrun, co-president of the Udacity MOOC, argues this very straightforwardly, explicitly and seemingly unashamedly. Interviewed in *Wired* magazine on 20 March 2012, he stated that the MOOC – such as his own Udacity – will indeed mean the eradication of universities, predicting that, in fifty years, there will only be ten of them left worldwide.

It is not just the future of the university that is at stake, however, it is the future of democratic dialogue and of widened participation in the social, political, cultural and economic franchise that is at stake. We have a duty, then, towards the future, and a duty that essentially forms part of an intergenerational ethical and social demand.

2.7 WHO PAYS? WHOSE DEBT?

In our current predicament, we have arrived at a situation where we face a more or less explicit narrowing of the range of engagement, combined with a narrowing of the range of people who can direct our historical future, but a gain in speed of return. Pushed to its logical limit, this kind of thing has its corollary in all those 'degrees' that one can buy at the press of a button on the web. You hand over your fee and, instantly, you get your return. Not only is this corrupt ethically, it also raises questions of justice and the freedom of the human agent, that 'gap' in time, that moment 'between past and future' that Arendt identifies not just with thought but also with the possibility of a force for freedom.

The UK government's current Minister for Higher Education, David Willetts, produced a book in 2010 called *The Pinch*. The argument of the book is that the post-Second World War generation, the so-called 'baby boomers', have done very well for themselves. They are born into fortunately propitious times and 'have concentrated wealth in the hands of their own generation'.[16] The issue for Willetts is that there is a danger that this generation has benefited not just from its inherited past, but also from the fact that it has stolen the future of its own children. We have had a good time, he argues, but now the bills are starting to come in, and it's the next generation – our children – who are being asked to pay them. This is a political situation: as he puts it, 'Good government values the future; bad government takes from it'.

The great puzzle, of course, is that in the very same year that this book appeared, Willetts himself as a government minister advocated what his own book calls 'bad government'. The new structure that is to finance university education, as of 2010 and the decisions of the Coalition government in the United Kingdom, is that the state will divest itself of financial interest in higher education, and therefore devolve its costs on to students themselves, as private individuals who will suffer extensive financial debts (at unpredictable rates of interest) as they have to pay enormously high tuition fees for their programmes of study. Meanwhile Willetts himself and the rest of the baby-boomer generation who sit in government thereby divest themselves of the need for investment in the future of their children and continue, in effect, to steal from them and from the future.

As has now been well documented, there are massive problems associated with the tuition fee arrangements. These have already been experienced elsewhere, in (for the obvious example) the massive personal debts that have engulfed the US system and that have threatened the future prospects of large numbers of individuals. In the United Kingdom, a typical three-year degree will incur personal debts of £27,000 (at 2014 prices), not to mention the added actual living costs, which can reach easily to a further £33,000 (approximately £7000 per annum for accommodation and £4000 per annum maintenance

---

[16] David Willetts, *The Pinch* (Atlantic Books, London, 2010), 1.

and general living costs). After three years, during which one might have been enjoying a salary, the student instead has a debt of around £60,000. Assume a below-average salary of, say, £18,000 per annum, and the total opportunity cost is some £114,000.

That, however, is not all. In the current arrangements, the student will only be eligible to repay the debt once they start earning £21,000 per annum. For Willetts and his allies, this represents a kind of justice and fairness. We might note, though, that £21,000 per annum is still some £5000 or so short of the average annual UK salary, and we might also note that the current arrangements mean that, for everything above £21,000, the student will have to pay an extra 9% tax, deducted at source, to repay the debt. If the student is fortunate enough to earn over £32,011 per annum, they will start to pay tax at the rate of 49%. In the coalition government's budget, the year after this arrangement was put in place, the UK Chancellor, George Osborne, reduced tax (from 50% to 45%) on all annual income above £150,000 per annum.

The student in this instance becomes the highest-rated taxpayer in the country. However, not all students will be in this fortunate position, especially in a social situation where jobs are precarious and scarce and where there are now very large numbers of extremely well-qualified students trying to find employment. There will therefore be many who do not qualify at all to make any repayments of their debt. This means that the next generation, if they are fortunate to be in employment, will not only be paying for their own university education retrospectively, but they will also be bailing out the government's debts that have been incurred by other, less fortunate students.

This is still not all. It is the government's intention to privatize these debts and to sell-off the loan-book. In the contractual agreement that every student must sign, in order to incur the tuition fee debt in the first place, the not-very-small print explains that the rate of interest payable is not guaranteed and may rise without notice. As and when a private company buys the loan-book, and raises the level of interest payable on the loan, the next generation will be facing what is essentially a retrospective hike in the already highly inflated tuition fees themselves.

This is entirely the wrong kind of debt, for it is part of a system of privatization of the public good that a university education actually is. It is designed to transfer the commonly shared wealth of public goods into the private hands of a small number of already wealthy people. Usually, this is called 'theft', but governments prefer to refer to it – for obvious ethical reasons – as 'privatization' or 'marketization' and 'competition'.

On 19 April 2011, Michael Arthur (who was at that time the Vice-Chancellor of Leeds University, Chair of the Russell Group and Board Member of Universities UK), took part in a debate on tuition fees on Channel 4 News. In October 2010, he had argued that the maximum fee he would charge at Leeds was £7500 per annum, and he stressed that students should remember that 'There's no up-front fee'. However, by the time of the TV debate (available at: http://www.youtube.com/watch?v=00hfQCfy5a8) he had moved to the permitted maximum of £9000, which, he argued, would allow for 'investment' (and which thus represented *more* than the actual costs of tuition). David Willetts described the system as 'fair and progressive' and suggested that an extra 9% in tax was 'reasonable' for an income over £21,000 (though he would later agree with his own chancellor that an extra 10% on income above £150,000 was unreasonable).

Challenged by two sixth-form pupils (Emma Weedon and Maryam Obeid), Michael Arthur defended the new regime as 'fairer' than any other available mode of financing university education. He gave figures: once earning £25,000, he said, the student would repay an extra £30 per month in addition to all her other tax and salary-related deductions, saying that this was 'the price of two movie tickets' in London. Since that time, Michael Arthur has moved to London, where he is now the Vice-Chancellor and Provost of University College London. When at Leeds, his total salary was £320,000 per annum (including £60,000 pension contributions that the university made for him). In London, now, his salary is higher, and, like many VCs, there are the added benefits of housing, cars, staff and so on.

In the light of his Channel 4 debate comments, here is a reasonable challenge: empty all of Michael Arthur's bank accounts, remove all of his other capital assets, put a debt of £114,000 in place of all of this and give him a job – in London – at £25,000. After a year of this, examine his knowledge of contemporary cinema.

Notwithstanding his defence of the regime, he had also indicated that no one in the university sector welcomed it and had asked David Willetts whether the proportions of state-interest and individual debt might be recalibrated if the nation's finances were to improve. However, if the system were indeed the fairest imaginable, then why would he want any such recalibration? He may also have forgotten that it was the Russell Group, of which he was Chair, that argued vociferously *for* this new regime.

In the end, that is not too surprising, as the Russell Group is, of course, part of that same arrangement whereby inequalities are to be made systemic. Not long after this, Michael Arthur also argued that it was a waste of money to spread research income around the whole sector, and he argued that it should effectively all be transferred to a small number of elite – that is, Russell Group – institutions.

It is here that we start to see the real consequences of 'shorting' in the university sector. The audit-efficiency model, grounded in the marketization of the university, yields a result where the sector becomes a primary agent of a drive towards inequalities. Those inequalities are not just inequalities of wealth, but also of opportunity and of participation in the society, and, further, this now increasingly anorexic participation in society refers not just to the society of today but also that of tomorrow. In short, the marketized university becomes the site in which intellectual and cultural capital is financialized and monetized; this in turn constructs the university as a prime agent of neo-liberal politics.

The result is increased debt for those among us who are least well endowed and the consequent reinvigoration of a social and class stratification that ensures that the wealthy – the elite 1%, the Russell Group and the CEOs – protect themselves and their status at the cost of everyone else. Inequality, such as this, destroys the social contract and it destroys the collegium and collective responsibilities that should be at the heart of the university. Theft such as this has no place in a university.

2.8 OBLIGATIONS

In conclusion, and by way of a bridge to my next chapter, I have here stressed the idea of a collegium as it relates to time. Fundamental to the idea of being-together, however, is a yet more fundamental question: 'who is my neighbour?'

My neighbour is the one in whom I place trust, but trust that is realized in actual and concrete material historical engagement. That is to say, the neighbour is she or he who introduces me to time, to the possibility of a future that is shaped by our acting together, collectively. In his great study of friendship and love, *Politiques de l'amitié*, Derrida argues that love and friendship are not just relations that bring people together in space, they also involve those lovers or friends in a temporal engagement with each other. This is for the simple reason that one can be loved and not know it, while one must always know that one loves, and therefore, the lover is always 'in advance of' the beloved.

The sophistication of this – and thus the very possibilities of friendship, love and even neighbourliness – is lost on those who consider the university as a marketplace of commodities, those static modules that 'contain' truths or essential facts. We might recall the extremely respectable philosophical tradition in which learning and love are allied, from Plato's *Symposium* all the way through to Badiou and his determination to see love as having a fundamental relation not just to truth but also to science and mathematics in particular.

Wilkinson and Pickett consider the relations between, on one hand, social status, and, on the other, friendship. In their research in *The Spirit Level*, they keep finding the two cropping up together, as if they are some kind of non-identical twins. In exploring this, they find that social status and friendship 'represent the two opposite ways in which human beings can come together'. The first, social status, operates in a mode of stratification, 'like ranking systems or pecking orders among animals', and they yield 'orderings based on power and coercion, on privileged access to resources, regardless of others' needs'. Putting this in its shockingly honest form, they write that 'In its most naked and animal form, might is right and the weakest eat least' (p. 199).

By contrast with this, friendship relations are almost completely the opposite. Friendship, they write, 'is about reciprocity, mutuality, sharing, social obligations and co-operation and recognition of each other's needs' (p. 200). This offers us a question: do we want a university system that is grounded in the kinds of social obligations – duties and debts – that are 'friendly' or do we want a system that encourages a darkly unethical situation where 'might is right' and where duty or any obligation of care towards others is simply deemed irrelevant? Do we want cooperation or league-table world-ranking competition? The former has an ethical foundation and the latter is of dubious morality.

The university, we might say by way of conclusion here, is the site where friendship, love and neighbourliness are all made possible, and they are made possible in a realization of secularity – that is, in a realization that the future of a society depends upon a basic realization that, *contra* Margaret Thatcher, there is indeed such a thing as society and, further, that its future existence depends on how we articulate and shape our being together.

That is to say: the university describes and founds a conception of citizenship and counters the capitalist drive to atomization of individuals and fragmentation of the social itself through its regular practices of 'divide and rule'. That is my next chapter.

3
CITIZENS, DENIZENS AND COSMOPOLITANS

If I were pressed to say why I love him, I feel that my only reply could be: 'Because it was he, because it was I'.

(Montaigne, 'On Friendship', p. 96)

3.1 ON THE PRODUCTION OF GLOBAL CITIZENS

Virtually every university institution nowadays presents itself as somehow shaped or determined in its fundamental values and activities by globalization. Most simply put, the language deployed is one where we are being enjoined to 'produce' what the institutions often refer to as 'global citizens'. The language itself is revealing; but it is revealing not just of an ideology, but also of some fundamental confusions or even contradictions.

That the university 'produces' something is interesting: if it produces, there must be a 'product'. In this specific case, the graduate – a human being to whom we have 'added value' through the addition of what was once called 'graduatedness' – is our 'product'. And, according to the preceding logic of neo-liberal economics, she or he carries the brand with them, like a label on an item of clothing: as with 'made in China', say, so also 'made in Stanford', 'a Cambridge double-starred First', or – in earlier times – an Oxford 'Gentleman's Third' or the jocular 'Bishop Desmond' (a 2:2).

Yet this is a bizarre way to think of human beings. Marx, in the 19th century, thought of production as being fundamental to human activity. In *The German Ideology* (1845–1846), he argued that we distinguish ourselves from animals with one clearly distinctive trait: production. We produce our means of subsistence, and thereby, at least indirectly, we produce our 'actual material life'. But is this what is meant by the contemporary use of this term, when universities claim that it is they who 'produce' graduates, and not the graduates who produce themselves and their own autonomous lives?

It seems clear that essentially today's usage is almost the precise contrary of Marx's. Marx was talking about autonomy, about our production of ourselves as autonomous people, people capable (literally) of 'giving ourselves the laws' – *autos nomos* – according to which we will organize ourselves in ways that keep us alive in the world. This, of course, is not straightforward, for, as he argued some five years later at the opening of his *Eighteenth Brumaire* (Marx, 1852), people do indeed make their own history, but they do not do so under conditions of their own choosing. Giving oneself the laws by which we live immediately engages the individual in a civic community that can agree to share those laws, and, further, the possibilities of our free agency in giving ourselves the laws are conditioned by what, in our history and past, has shaped and formed us.

In this case, therefore, the production involves precisely the kind of negotiations – the always ongoing and developing negotiations – of past with present. That negotiation is oriented towards an ever-changing future. Yet, as I have shown in previous chapters, it is the very pliability of this, the mutability of that negotiation, that is denied by the marketization and commodification of knowledge – to which is now added the marketization and commodification of students themselves, as 'products' of a machinery that 'delivers' workers and consumers to the social formation. Just as knowledge is reduced and eviscerated, to the point where it becomes information and then data, likewise our student is reduced to the status of human resource in the service of human capital. The university becomes – as in the fabled myth so eloquently attacked by Stefan Collini – the widget-factory, and the student becomes the graduate who is 'designed' as a 'product' to fit some existing machinery. Organizations such as the Confederation of British Industries refer to this as 'job-readiness' or the 'work-ready graduate'.

In passing, this might itself offer an explanation for why it is that so many business organizations complain about the Higher Education (HE) sector. If the university produces something that fits the existing machinery, business – which needs constantly new machinery for a necessarily changing commercial world (i.e. for a secular and historical business-sector) – inevitably falls behind in any commercial competition. One cannot 'produce' innovation as if it, too, were a simple commodity, however; one can only encourage a state of intellectual affairs in which a disposition towards curiosity and inventiveness – research and imaginative thinking – becomes more normative.

The business cliché, of course, is that the business and commercial sectors (at least in the corporate business world) want people who 'think outside the box', not realizing that this very phrase itself, as a mindless cliché, is precisely a thinking from *within* the constricting box of managerialist jargon, a jargon that ensures that systems of managerialism actually constrict and replace the need for proper managing itself. Those who present themselves as thinking 'outside the box' actually thereby demonstrate precisely the extent to which they have been incorporated 'within the box' of conformist, restricted and restrictive managerialist practice. The very language of 'production', with respect to the university sector, is in many fundamental ways intrinsically damaging to the activities and work of students, teachers and researchers.

It is, however, the second contradiction that will be of most interest here: the oxymoronic phrase 'global citizen'. By definition, a citizen is an individual who is affiliated in some profound way with a specific nation state, or, historically, a city state. Etymologically, the term suggests membership of a very specific location, in a city; and, in terms of that etymology, at least as derived from the Roman usage of the *civitas*, the word 'citizen' means 'a freeman of the city'. The globe, however, is very definitely not a city but a world, and thus 'global citizenship' suggests a difficult conflation of two different kinds of social or political affiliation.

One might think of persons, however, as being affiliated to a city or nation state not just by natality or birth, but by adoption and choice. After all, I have laid much emphasis throughout this book on the idea of alterity, of making things foreign in some way and of attending, through Sennett's 'empathy', to difference and to others. We may therefore need a word for this political condition in which we adopt or choose our affiliation, and we already have one: a 'denizen' is precisely a foreigner who not only has adopted an affiliation to a country that she or he has chosen, but one who, by that very choice, is also admitted to the existing rights of membership of the place. A denizen is, as it were, a 'naturalized citizen', a foreigner who is afforded the same rights as those of the citizen-by-birth. As discussed in Chapter 1, so also here we have a regulation of the competing demands of the force of nature (birth) and the force of circumstance (culture or history), and these meet in the denizen.

Perhaps, though, what the university branding and marketing officers and advertising agents mean by the phrase 'global citizen' is something like an individual who is characterized more by her or his 'cosmopolitanism'. Once again, if we consider the language carefully here, we find some problems and difficulties. A cosmopolitan is one who is not only knowledgeable about many parts of the world beyond the geographical part in which she or he actually lives out their material and biological existence, but she or he is also one who is thereby freed from precise and identifiable national affiliations. The word derives from Greek: *kosmos* = world; *politēs* = citizen. It follows, then, that, by definition, the cosmopolitan is actually at odds with the citizen: while the citizen acknowledges her or his affiliation to a nation state, as does also the denizen, the cosmopolitan – the global citizen – is precisely she or he who denies, or who at least severely limits the effects of, those affiliations.

If we look for an example of this, we might alight on the case of someone like Rupert Murdoch, who starts as an Australian citizen, but when that is commercially inconvenient for his American business interests, becomes a denizen of the United States and adopts American citizenship. The next stage, formally, would be one whereby he is equally prepared to jettison American citizenship in turn for something else to which a yet more fundamental affiliation – and one that is *not grounded in any nation* – is established; perhaps something like the affiliation to capital itself – which can be located anywhere, and is thus cosmopolitan – and to capital acquisition. Or perhaps it implies affiliation to something non-located, non-terrestrial, such as satellite TV or some similar 'virtual' place from which the value of 'virtue' can be eliminated.

Let us assume, for the moment, that the 'global' university does not see its primary task as being the 'production' of Murdoch clones (though that may, in fact, be the unstated and tacit normative case). Perhaps, more obviously, one of the issues here is how the university might regulate the competing demands, or adjudicate the ostensibly opposing claims, of local citizenship and global responsibilities. Interestingly, one sees similar things happening at a micro-level in the organization of university faculties themselves. It used to be the case that colleagues affiliated to their 'discipline', which brought an identification with a 'department'. However, one of the (possibly unintended) consequences of the much-vaunted 'interdisciplinarity' of recent times has been precisely the breaking of any such affiliations. The strength of a discipline or of a department is thus vitiated: either departments become simple agglomerates of atomized individuals (who can be divided and ruled, and where they can be co-opted for structures of 'competition' in which individual self-advancement trumps collegial pursuit), or they are 'dissolved' into loose arrangements of 'schools' or 'colleges', where – paradoxically – collegial affiliations are also weakened, their power dispersed and without sustained focus and realigned instead with a vertical power structure.

Beyond the walls of the institution, we can find similar effects. The term 'cosmopolite' has always been contentious. As Alan B. Farmer notes, the earliest usage of the term – earlier than that in 1598 acknowledged by the OED – is in John Dee's 1577 text, *General and Rare Memorials Pertayning to the Perfect Arte of Navigation*. Farmer shows that the usage of the term at that time was very profoundly ambivalent. On one hand, it operated as we tend to consider it nowadays, whereby a cosmopolitan is one who seeks greater knowledge through travel to diverse parts of the world. However, on the other hand, its usage is extremely disparaging, describing 'a base sinner who delights in worldly pleasures like fighting, feasting, cheating, and whoring'.[1]

One has to assume it's the former definition that the contemporary university has in mind – at least consciously. However, it is interesting to note, in passing, the tacit nod to the latter and less flattering definition. In the logic of 'competition' as an alleged primary driver of quality, and in the concept of a 'global race' in which UK Prime Minister Cameron has entered the United Kingdom as a competitor, institutions do indeed 'fight' for place, 'feast' or celebrate achievements when they win, 'cheat' in the manipulation of figures and statistics. ('Whoring' might be different, of course, at least in its literal sense.) If Cameron is right in asserting the need to win in the 'global race', is it really the case that he explicitly wants other nations and other people to be 'losers'? Can he seriously mean what he says? If so, then the ethics of this global race can surely be questioned – unless, of course, one subscribes to an ideology designed to justify increased disparities of wealth or life-chances, and to justify those disparities through a subscription to increased inequality among 'citizens'. If this is a questionable ethics in international relations, it is surely all the more questionable when translated and transferred into the university sector. Any president or VC who wants to enter into a competitiveness that means that students in other institutions will be losers should seriously examine their conscience.

The divergent views of the cosmopolitan outlined by Farmer fundamentally related to and even arose from the affiliations – often or primarily a religious affiliation – of the speaker, and, in the 16th and 17th centuries in Europe, these religious affiliations also pertained to the identity and characterization of the nation state in which the speaker found herself or himself, as Catholic, Protestant (and sometimes as Jewish, Muslim and 'Moorish') and certainly sectarian in some way. Oddly, then, 'cosmopolitan' as a word is itself not very cosmopolitan but is rather conditioned by what is essentially a fundamentalist sectarianism.

---

[1] Alan B. Farmer (2007) 'Cosmopolitanism and foreign books in early modern England', *Shakespeare Studies* XXXV: 61.

In our own days, my contention is that it is conditioned by a sectarian *political* choice 'for' neo-liberal globalization, a choice that systematically eviscerates citizenship itself of any meaningful substance or historical power. Our current 'sectarian cosmopolitanism', if I can coin that usage, constitutes an attack on autonomy and also, thereby, on human freedom and its possibilities. The emerging question is why the university sanctions this, rather than exposing, discussing and even critiquing it.

3.2 BANKERS, MIGRANTS AND CIVIC COMMITMENT

Politics – like 'even the President of the United States' – 'sometimes must have to stand naked', as Bob Dylan sang prophetically in *It's all right Ma* (Dylan, 1965), where 'money doesn't talk, it swears'. In the wake of the 2008 near-global financial crash, nation states were faced with a substantial economic and political predicament. As George W. Bush put it when news of the collapse of Lehman Brothers came through, 'This sucker could go down', meaning that the whole financial sector might crumble. The response worldwide was to support the financial sector, especially the large banks, through a massive injection of government support or, more accurately put, a massive injection of funds that national governments receive through the taxation of their citizens.

Bankers essentially held nation states to ransom, threatening that if they did not get this support – and, yet more importantly – if they did not get support to continue to be paid wildly extravagant salaries and bonuses, regardless of performance, the 'suckers' would indeed 'go down', ensuring massive increases in unemployment, repossessions of houses, foreclosures on loans and emptying of the pension-pots to which individual citizens had contributed substantial amounts of their own funds or earnings. Further, the bankers would simply 'jump ship', leave the country in question and work elsewhere, in jurisdictions where there was looser regulation, higher pay and bonus structures, and where their own 'burden' of taxation would be reduced, such that their 'compensation' would be higher in real terms.

The language is revealing. These see tax not as a measure of our commitment to a society, but as a burden that they have to bear, and they see salaries as 'compensation', as if the very fact of work was some kind of intrinsic and fundamental personal inconvenience whose vulgar demands have somehow damaged them in ways that require other civic taxpayers to make amends for the insult that asks them to work for a salary, or that dares to tax them proportionately, like other citizens.

The bank executives, then, are 'global citizens' in the sense that they have no affiliation to the nations – or to the citizens who comprise those nations – that supported them. They benefited post-2008 from a form of corporate welfare, and, despite having wrecked whole economies, having destroyed the personal savings of millions and having essentially robbed people of their pensions and investments, they now continue to be rewarded for these failures, through taxes on the general population of other citizens. One way of thinking about tax, of course, is that it is precisely a kind of debt, a 'duty' or bond that commits an individual to a shared enterprise or community, and it is tax – that very duty or commitment to the social sphere – that the global-citizen-banker is avoiding, thus distancing herself or himself from the community, even when that very community sustains the bankers' lifestyles.

For universities, there is one major consequence of a tolerance of this ransom-demand. In December 2010, in the United Kingdom, the costs of university tuition were substantially transferred into private hands, as a government – for the first time – required the students of its nation to become massively indebted personally for a university education. The tripling of tuition fees was accompanied by a systematic withdrawal of all state support (a 100% cut) for teaching on arts, humanities and social sciences; as if this particular nation state had no need for or financial interest in the civic constituency, largely constituted by arts and culture, itself.

Indicative of the difference here, and of the priorities that the university shares, is the following statistic: in December 2010, Barclays Bank announced its executive bonus-pot as £1.6bn. That sum is just under 33% of the *total* funding for the entire university sector nationwide provided by government for our teaching in arts, humanities and social sciences. Thus, one bank is deemed to weigh more, in terms of its substantial and symbolic value, than some 150 universities and many thousands of students. December 2010 is also the date of the great betrayal, when the UK coalition government tripled university tuition fees despite a pre-election signed public pledge by Liberal Democrats, now in coalition, to abolish fees entirely. The university sector, in the form of Universities UK but led primarily by the Russell Group of Vice-Chancellors, officially welcomed this, and, in doing so, they made the universities complicit with these priorities. Essentially, in December 2010 the sector leadership agreed that the arts, humanities and social sciences – unlike the STEM subjects – were not important enough economically, politically, socially or culturally to warrant the State's financial interest. In short, they 'de-civilized' these faculties, and they did so in compliance with a government dedicated to increasing disparities of wealth and to increasing structural inequalities in civic society, 'justifying' this by reference to competition in the face of alleged austerity.

Against the form of financial global mobility enjoyed by the banking and financial sector, we might set a different form of mobility: migration and immigration, sometimes forced and therefore conditioned by refugee status. While bankers assert their power and hold citizens of nation states to ransom, governments – above all in the United Kingdom but also elsewhere – stigmatize the global (and sometimes forced) mobility of workers or students who move precisely because they are poor, menaced by their domestic governments, tortured or threatened environmentally by corporate commercial interests. New immigration rules are established, the effect of which is precisely to prevent these poor from becoming global citizens, and, instead of being lauded for their enterprise and for the risks they take in migrating, the poor of the world are instead characterized as welfare cheats, health-tourists, scroungers and skivers. Not for these the welfare that has been given in excessive amounts to bankers; rather, from these, what little they have is to be taken away.

The hypocritical attitude described here is precisely as described in Matthew, 13:12, where Matthew describes Jesus justifying his use of parables. The parable, as Kermode argued in *The Genesis of Secrecy*, is essentially divisive: for the elect 'in the know', it confirms their knowledge; for the excluded 'outside', it confirms their place outside. Parables are not for understanding, not available to hermeneutic critique. They just are, and, logically, therefore, it follows that 'whosoever hath, to him shall be given, and he shall have more abundance: but whosoever hath not, from him shall be taken away even that he hath'. The logic, once again, is the logic of a force of nature, 'This is this', and a class division is established between the privileged insiders and those condemned always to remain outside. The contemporary parallel is the divide between the 1% and the 99%, between the bankers and the refugees. 'Elect' means 'elite'.

This happens notwithstanding the fact that all the evidence demonstrates that immigrants typically benefit the economy of a nation state, and that they pay more in tax than they cost in any form of welfare or social benefit. Above all, their 'denizen' rights are challenged, as the opportunity to benefit from the rights afforded to citizens are challenged by precisely the same governments who have robbed the poor and indebted their student-citizen constituencies, not to mention future generations, to subsidize the extraordinary income of bank and other corporate-sector or private-sector executives. Tacitly, the force of nature (citizenship by birth and genetic inheritance) is given free rein, not countered by any tempering force of civilization.

Worst of all: universities – and perhaps above all those that pride themselves on their branding as 'global' or 'world-class' (whatever that might actually mean) have been co-opted into this process. Given the economic need to recruit high-fee paying migrant students, universities applaud themselves on their cosmopolitan nature. In this case, 'globalization' works by allowing advanced economies to draw funds away from developing economies and gaining the benefit of the talents of the citizens of those other less-advanced nations and economies.

Further, in fact, the extremely negative and subversive result of this migration is that the sector, especially in the United Kingdom, has been charged with the policing strategy of 'monitoring' students and ensuring that they are occupied fully in their studies and not doing anything else. The process stems from what was essentially a near-racist form of so-called anti-terrorist legislation, in which it is the 'non-EU' (sometimes code for 'non-white') foreigner who is to be monitored; but, given that this potentially is indeed racist in singling out individuals from particular jurisdictions, it has to circumvent both anti-racist and also other potentially discriminatory and anti-equality legislation. Rather than reject it, however, it is instead applied to *all* students equally in the name of supposed 'equality' legislation. All are now equally suspect.

That is to say: all students are finding that their rights, as citizens, are being denied them in some fundamental respects. It is as if the condition of being a student itself approximates, in the eyes of some governments (and perhaps above all, to the UK government), to the condition of being a potential terrorist. The cops are on campus, and academics are being required to don the uniform. This is hardly conducive to the establishment of good citizenship, and the potential damage that it does to the trust necessary for the intellectual exploration of ideas and thought is enormous.

Put philosophically, we could say that that which is foreign is no longer permitted, and this encompasses 'foreign' thinking, any form of thinking that is 'outside-the-box' to the extent that it is 'outside the nation' or simply outside the ideological and fundamentalist norms that govern what counts, for governments, as 'natural' – that is, any thought that counters an alleged 'natural' or 'genetic' elitism. And, as the example of Barclays against universities UK above shows, the university sector's leadership has led us to a position where that which is deemed 'natural' or (in their preferred term) 'realistic' is the establishment and validation of massive inequality as the proper condition of our social being together. We are coming close to the situation in which the university exists to demand and to produce 'conformity', the effect of which is to deny what it is that universities are fundamentally for: the possibility of thinking itself.

We have entered the world of the 'household spies' of Orwell's *1984*, and the university sector is increasingly complicit with this nefarious state of affairs. There are two major aspects of this that are of interest for the current argument: first, university education is increasingly aligned with surveillance and control, and second, university education is becoming structurally integral to a society of increasing inequalities of wealth, grounded in an attack on citizenship.

3.3 ON COMPETITION, OR THE LEGITIMIZATION OF SYMBOLIC VIOLENCE

At issue here is a fundamental matter of neighbourliness. Who is the 'neighbour' in any community, and what might it mean to have relations with that which is adjacent to ourselves, that which neighbours our boundaries? What might it mean to have commitments, as social citizens of a polity, with our neighbours?

Ha-Joon Chang has adopted the phrase 'Bad Samaritans' to describe the kind of bad international relations that have shaped contemporary economies across the international domain. He outlines how Korea emerged historically as a very powerful economy, but from an astonishingly low baseline. For what he calls the neo-liberal economics establishment, the story of Korea is a story of the success of free trade, of marketization and of private sector dynamism. However, the facts are actually at odds with this series of claims. Korea got to its present powerful position largely through state intervention, which helped to direct and to kick-off economic success. Chang shows how 'The Korean economic miracle was the result of a clever and pragmatic mixture of market incentives and state direction', and he goes on to situate Korea as a nation that essentially tried to find a good means of regulating the claims of private and public goods and activities: 'While it took markets seriously, the Korean strategy recognized that they often needed to be corrected through policy intervention'.[2]

In line with the arguments advanced separately by Mariana Mazzucato, in her 2011 study of *The Entrepreneurial State*, Chang's further claim is that Korea is not an exception in any way in this; rather, he argues, every successful economy has followed this similar route: essentially a mixed economy, with roles for both markets and for state interventions. Mazzucato pointed out the extremely important role played by the state in proactive research strategy. She asks questions that need no answer, such as 'how many people know that the algorithm that led to Google's success was funded by a public sector National Science Foundation grant? Or that molecular antibodies, which provided the foundation for biotechnology before venture capital moved into the sector, were discovered in public Medical Research Council labs in the UK'.[3]

This version of events, however, is far from the prevailing narratives within a neo-liberal economics establishment, grounded in the orthodoxy that Joseph

---

[2] Ha-Joon Chang, *Bad Samaritans* (Random House, 2008), 15.

[3] Mazzucato, *Entrepreneurial State* (Demos, London, 2011), 19.

Stiglitz, among others, has called 'market fundamentalism'. That orthodoxy sets up an entirely false dichotomy between private sector activity (good) and public sector activity (bad, evil), and this Manichean opposition, recast in precisely moralizing terms as a battle between good and evil, also aligns this kind of thinking with other fundamentalisms, especially those grounded in the moralities of religions. This may be why the 'bad Samaritan' metaphor is so powerful, in fact.

Chang's 'neighbourly' question in the face of all this, then, is 'why don't the rich countries recommend to today's developing countries the strategies that served them so well?' (Chang, pp. 15–16). His answer is that the rich countries are not just in thrall to the ideological lies spoken by neo-liberal market fundamentalism, but also that they are essentially very bad neighbours: 'Today, there are certainly some people in the rich countries who preach free market and free trade to the poor countries in order to capture larger shares of the latter's markets and to pre-empt the emergence of possible competitors. They ... act as "Bad Samaritans", taking advantage of others who are in trouble' (Chang, p. 16).

This formulation recalls Jimmy Reid's historic Rectorial Address in the University of Glasgow in 1972. In that great speech, which the *New York Times* compared favourably with Lincoln's Gettysburg Address, Reid argued explicitly against the logic of 'competitiveness' and aggressive individualism in university and society alike.[4] He argued that a university education is a preparation for life, and not just for jobs. Indeed, it is by now abundantly clear that the transformation of our universities, worldwide, into elevated 'finishing-schools' whose graduates are primarily geared towards taking up their 'human capital' and 'human resource' role is a massive impoverishment of the sector, of education and of any sense of a university ideal. The university's potential is eviscerated, becoming instead just a service to provide fodder for a specific economic programme. Students become precisely that fodder, and the very idea of them being 'citizens' is entirely lost under their new title as 'human capital' (as when they are on unpaid internships) or 'human resource' (if they find paid employment). When the university is reduced to the function of preparation for jobs and not for life, life itself gets lost under the jobs. Citizenship becomes irrelevant, except to the extent that it is characterized by or identified solely with market consumption.

It is also important to recall that Reid's great argument derived, of course, precisely from a position that had also been intent on protecting jobs: his role

---

[4] The speech is available at: http://www.scottishleftreview.org/li/index.php?option=com_content&task=view&id=336.

as a trade union leader was one where, instead of opting for a strike action, he organized instead a work-in on the Upper Clyde's shipyards at a time when, in the interests of an alleged 'efficiency' that was later exposed as a cover for ideological determinations by government, the employers themselves went on a kind of strike, with a lockout of the workforce: a direct form of 'enclosure' of the shipyards, in which the employers attempted to deny workers the right to work at all. It was akin to 'suspension' as a disciplinary device discussed earlier. Reid knew of the dignity of work, and of its importance for our collegial membership of a community – citizenship; but he saw education and, especially, university education as something that encompassed work, and more besides.

It is of the essence of a university education, he argued, that we should learn to reject both 'the false morality' of a rat race that blunts our critical faculties, and the competitiveness-ideology that 'would caution silence in the face of injustice lest you jeopardize your chances of promotion and self-advancement'. This should also be recalled in the context of governments and administrations, such as the UK coalition 2010–2015 and their predecessors of some 40 years, who believe that markets and competition – the rat race of aggressive self-advancement, necessarily at the cost of the security of others – should be the key driver of the university sector as a whole.

The obvious examples of Chang's Bad Samaritans are to be found, in our contemporary economies, in the ways in which the 'Troika' (European Commission, IMF, European Central Bank) has dealt with the post-2008 crisis, especially as it has affected the Euro-zone. Ireland, Greece, Spain, Portugal all found out that their budgets were essentially being set by determinations stemming from Angela Merkel's German financial model – and that these budgets were essentially being imposed upon the citizens of these nations. The Greeks likewise were forced into adopting economic policies with which at least significant and substantial constituencies (who were not to be trusted with a consultation) disagree fundamentally. In Greece, as also in Italy, unelected technocratic elites were put in power, and they were put in power over a population that – in a crude and straightforward bypassing of democratic structures and participation – were not to be consulted about matters that affected adversely their very existence.

Citizens of these nations had legitimate interests in these matters, but those interests were denied them, and the result, in some cases, led to a state of affairs where the adoption of these policies caused the death of citizens who, in need of medical prescriptions, were denied access to their medication after suffering financial strictures. Avner Offer, in 'A Warrant for Pain', has worked through the economics of this, by introducing ethical issues into the economic considerations that govern, for his key example, US healthcare provision.[5] The argument – which in healthcare issues is literally a matter of life and death – is that a 'duty of care' towards others has to act as an effective counterweight to neo-liberal economics. Neo-liberalism works if and only if both parties to a transaction have full and complete knowledge of all aspects of the transaction in question, and this, though possible in abstract terms, has no bearing on how things actually work. If economics triumphs over ethics, then death can be the result – and so, neoliberalism has its 'warrant for pain', including pain that leads to death.

Leaving aside the extreme here – the actual death of citizens – we nonetheless have a current predisposition that leads to the systemic denial of citizenship to people who find themselves at odds with an economic orthodoxy whose credentials are themselves extremely dubious. In short, we might say that good citizenship – being a good neighbour or Good Samaritan – requires a strong regard for ethical considerations. The contemporary condition, crucially including the determination of university priorities, prefers instead to consider ethics only *after* issues of personal or private economic gain. Essentially, the university here is complicit with that form of 'meritocracy' that actually works to protect 'privilege'. It is that form of meritocracy that is grounded in 'just-world' theories that Offer shows to be consistent with classical liberal and neo-liberal economics. In 'just-world' theories, people get what they deserve. It follows, then, that if you are poor, it is your own fault and you are getting what you deserve. Likewise, if you are rich (or a member of the 1%), there is no further need – no need at all, in fact – to 'justify' yourself. Your worth is literally 'self-evident'.

In *How Much is Enough?*, Robert and Edward Skidelsky examine this in both academic and philosophical terms. They point out that, in our time, 'Economics is not just any academic discipline. It is the theology of our age, the language that all interests, high and low, must speak if they are to win a respectful hearing in the courts of power'.[6] This 'triumph of economics' in the university, they argue, has allowed economics to rise to its position of institutional authority because of the failure of other disciplines 'to impress their stamp on political debate' (Skidelsky and Skidelsky, p. 92). Indeed, my own argument here goes further: it is precisely the university as an institution that has failed wholly in this regard.

Further, in terms of the relation between economics and the wider issues of justice and of 'the good life', Skidelsky and Skidelsky point out that the

---

[5] Avner Offer, 'A warrant for pain', available at: http://weaethicsconference.files.wordpress.com/2012/03/offer-warranted-pain51b.pdf. See also: http://www.nuff.ox.ac.uk/economics/history/Paper102/offer102.pdf for original version, 'Caveat Emptor'.

[6] Robert and Edward Skidelsky, *How Much is Enough?* (Penguin, London, 2013), 92.

prevailing economics traditions 'forbid any *public* preference for this or that way of life' (Skidelsky and Skidelsky, p. 93). The idea of an intrinsically 'good life' has ceded place to a marketplace where we find and 'choose' from 'a range of *desired lifestyles*' (Skidelsky and Skidelsky, p. 89). This is a failing, they argue, because 'for a social species such as ours, the good life is essentially a life in common with others. Its home is not in the brains of individuals but in groups of people doing things together' (Skidelsky and Skidelsky, p. 93).

The contradiction for those partisans of meritocratic 'just-world' theories that subsume ethics under economics is obvious: if your value is so self-evident, why bother with the self-transformations that we usually call learning or education? In the logical extension of privatization of the sector, we not only close the university sector, but we also reduce citizenship – ostensibly something grounded in democratic participation in decision-making – to hierarchical and genetic privilege. Class and class-based privilege rule, and so-called 'social mobility' is the myth that allows this to persist. However, 'social mobility' is, as it were, the 'scandal' through which the occasional working-class individual finds herself occupying a middle-class social stratum, thus showing to all others that 'Yes, we can', 'it can be done' and 'it could be you'. Thus, social mobility, which exists for isolated cases, justifies the fundamental position that the underprivileged are getting what they deserve. The fact that a mere 85 of the world's richest individuals have a share of the world's wealth that is equivalent to the rest combined (i.e. they have 50% of the lot) does not trouble the neoliberal university at all. How is it possible that a university sector got itself into this position?

One possible answer is that the determinations of this lie not in crude economics, but rather in issues that are less directly financial. They have more to do with what Bourdieu called 'cultural capital' or 'intellectual capital' than with the straightforward flaunting of financial wealth. Wilkinson and Pickett follow this line in their *Spirit Level*, as they examine how issues of aesthetic taste – which one might properly see as a centrally constituent element of a university arts education – help to determine and to consolidate social elites (who subsequently acquire the lion's share of common wealth). 'Middle-class and upper-class people,' they write, 'have the right accents, know how to behave in "polite society", know that education can enhance their advantages. They pass this on to their children ... [and] This is how elites become established and maintain their elite status'.[7] This, however, is not simply a matter of self-regarding social distinctions, rather, it is socially corrosive for all concerned.

---

[7] Richard Wilkinson and Kate Pickett, *The Spirit Level* (revised edn, Penguin, London, 2010), 163.

Wilkinson and Pickett go on to point out that people use aesthetic taste – and an aesthetic education – certainly, as a marker of social distinction, 'but throughout the social hierarchy people also use discrimination and downward prejudice to prevent those below them from improving their status' (Wilkinson and Pickett, 163). Although we laud ideas of equality, the distinctions made by 'educated taste' work to 'keep people in their place'. As they point out, this is far from neutral: 'Bourdieu calls the actions by which the elite maintain their distinction *symbolic violence*; we might just as well call them discrimination and snobbery' (Wilkinson and Pickett, 164), and their view is that this form of class-based prejudice is similar to other forms of prejudice, such as racial prejudice, which we routinely condemn.

How have we reached a position where the university's education priorities can become complicit with social violence and genetic prejudice rather than with the public good of citizenship and neighbourliness?

3.4 THE OCCUPATION OF THE UNIVERSITY

We should consider further the value of neighbourliness, and the relation of the university as an institution to issues of citizenship and to globalization, in terms of this issue of costs, ownership, property and the proprieties of 'occupation'.

The university can be aligned with the civic state, or with the city state. In the city state, as David Harvey has shown, there is a question of right: the 'right to the city'. This is something that we have already seen dramatized in Shakespeare's *Coriolanus*, as I outlined that above, but it has a real political purchase deriving from the ancient *droit de la cité*.

In 2013 in London, there was an assertion of the 'right to the university'. Students occupied some university offices in protest against the privatization, marketization and outsourcing of services that they saw as endangering their educational infrastructure. This was one of what was becoming a long series of such occupations in various universities across the United Kingdom. This particular protest was also aligned with a pay dispute between the university and the academic staff. The university authorities invited the police on to the campus, and forcibly evicted the occupiers from the university, using the force of nature: violence. This time, though, this force of nature (violence) is now tied to politics, such that the State itself, in the form of the police, and now explicitly allied with 'the university' perpetrates and culturally 'legitimizes' this violence against students, the 'citizens of the university' as it were, and it does so in the name of 'the university'.

As Brenna Bhandar argued, in a blog for the *LRB* on 10 December 2013, this incident indicated a significant shift in the relations between universities and students. The university used an injunction secured from the High Court, prohibiting 'persons unknown (including students of the University of London)' from 'entering or remaining upon the campus and buildings of University of London for the purpose of occupational protest action' for the next six months. This, says Bhandar, relates directly to the current drive towards ideological and economic privatization of the sector and of its constituent elements. 'Injunctions,' she writes, 'are a private law remedy. They are being granted to prohibit protest as if universities, as legal persons, were like any other private property owner; as if students were like any people at large, violating the property rights of the university'. What is now happening is that 'By granting possession orders, courts are effectively turning student protesters into trespassers on their universities, liable to fines and imprisonment if they defy the injunctions in order to express dissent'.

In short: in this situation, students are no longer students and are certainly not allowed to have any thought that differs from or calls into question the prevailing orthodoxy of the university, as set by its 'owner', the VC. The VC of the University of London – in this instance Adrian Smith – has asserted his right to ownership not only of 'the university' and its buildings, but also of what constitutes legitimate thought or belief within those buildings. It is precisely the same issue as that faced by Jimmy Reid in 1972: a 'lock-out' and enclosure of the intellectual commons, through which the VC asserts his total control of the space, place and identity of 'the university'. Ideologically, it approximates to a condition of tyranny or, if that's too flavoursome a word, then we can settle on authoritarianism: the assertion of unearned authority used to coerce and intimidate others into subjugation.

This is exactly the same issue – the right to the city, the right to the university – as we saw in my earlier discussion of *Coriolanus*. There, the question was 'what is the city but the people', and here, the parallel question is 'what is the university but those who study there, the collegium?' For many (though not all) contemporary VCs and self-styled Presidents, however, 'the University, c'est moi'. The properly constitutional and earned legitimacy of an institution – its social 'authority', if you will – has been translated into unconstitutional and anti-democratic authoritarianism.

It is in this way that such VCs can assert their 'right' to identity precisely *as* the university. It recalls a medieval or early modern fiefdom, where earls and barons were identified precisely by their appropriation of and identification with land: 'Warwick', 'York', 'Cornwall', 'Essex' and so on. In the present day, this effectively structures the university as an institution scarred by a substantial cleavage and divide between an oligarchical and autocratic power, and a subservient class who are being denied participation in the life of the institution. In this, such sector leaders deny civic membership of the institution to its constituency of academics, students and ancillary or support staff.

One example will suffice to demonstrate what is at issue here. In the United Kingdom, we have 'mission groups', the most powerful of which is 'the Russell Group'. This group is usually referred to as a group *of universities*, and most people assume that there is, indeed, some type of arrangement here that implicates the staff of the participating institutions. However, this is factually untrue. The Russell Group is a membership organization consisting of a group of 24 individuals, being the VCs of each institution; the institutions themselves have absolutely no constitutional or legal affiliation to the group. It is constitutionally akin to an old-style 'gentleman's club', each of whose 24 members pays – from their institution's state-funding or financing – a personal membership fee (currently ca. £40,000 per person per annum). The group then claims or asserts the right not just to 'represent' their institutions, but to identify their own individual and personal views precisely as the agreed constitutional views of the institutions that they supposedly serve; but they do so without consultation, and with no mechanism whatsoever through which their separate constituencies have any constitutional rights to express a view on any issues of 'Russell Group policy'. Indeed, the danger now is that if an academic whose VC is a member of the Russell Group dares to criticize some Russell Group policy, they can be deemed *ipso facto* to be directly criticizing and even calling into question the authority of their own VC. This can be professionally risky, especially perhaps for less well-established academics. It is a form of institutional implicit bullying.

In short, a 'mission group' such as this is clearly identifiable as an oligarchy, and an oligarchy that is self-appointed, self-selecting and authoritarian. Membership – and recall that this is *personal* rather than institutional – is 'by invitation only'. The group is extremely powerful, and, quite apart from fracturing the sector that they are supposed to support, they have done irreparable damage to the idea of the university as a community of scholarship or a place for discussion and debate. There is no platform for debate over Russell Group policy, except within the walls of their offices where the members of the oligarchy talk to each other; and yet, the effects of the 'decisions' made in secret there affect the lives of thousands of staff, students and support-staff or ancillary colleagues. Paradoxically, while demanding increasing evidence of the massive benefits of the sector by requiring academic staff to increase the visibility of their 'public engagement' activities (i.e. our citizenship and commitment to our fellow citizens), these leaders – above all, the Russell Group of VCs – are themselves invisible in the public sphere, divorced entirely from it and from citizenship itself.

An oligarchy is fundamentally at odds with anything resembling a democracy, which would entail the participation of citizens working together for a common and public good. The oligarchy that increasingly shapes and dominates the university sector works to preserve itself and its privileges, even if, in order to do so, it has to deny citizenship as such.

And their pay – which, like CEOs in corrupt organizations, they essentially set for themselves through 'consultations' with or 'benchmarking against' other members of the oligarchy – is excessive and necessarily inflationary: each rise 'to keep up' raises the overall average, and requires further rises in turn, in a spiral of increases that distance these elites from material realities and from the daily life of their institutions. And now add Cicero's great rhetorical question: *cui bono*? Who benefits from this?

It is surely not merely coincidence that, in popular culture in these financially troubled and inegalitarian times, the figure of the vampire or of the pirate has become a key cultural figure (consider the success of the *Twilight* series of films, or of Johnny Depp's character, modelled on Keith Richards, in the *Pirates of the Caribbean* series). The vampire lives off the blood, sweat and labour of others, sustaining himself in vigour while draining others of the very force of life itself. The other key figure that may be relevant here is that of the zombie, not just in films but also in economics and in business itself. At the end of 2012, R3 (who represent insolvency businesses) indicated that, in the United Kingdom alone, there were around 146,000 'zombie businesses'.[8] Such organizations become parasitic upon the rest of the community to sustain them; but they themselves are unable to make any substantial contribution to a shared public good.

This is increasingly the situation into which the university sector is being forced: unable to contribute to the public good, hampered by a self-serving oligarchical and authoritarian elite who seek private gain and who validate personal economic greed as the key driver of economic and social success. Meanwhile, the exponential growth of consultancy-style organizations, themselves entirely parasitic upon the university sector's funds, continues to rise. Citizens lose their place to vampires, pirates and zombies.

3.5 ON THE SCANDALS OF SOCIAL MOBILITY

This is all entirely at odds with the idea of collaboration, or of establishing affiliations among a community. At the centre of this is the sense of growing

---

[8] See: 13 November 2012, Hugh Pym's report, available at: http://www.bbc.co.uk/news/business-20262282.

disengagement from the social and the fracturing of the political sphere itself, the shattering, indeed, of the very *politēs* that constitutes the citizen.

Richard Sennett argues that 'in capitalism, social cohesion is inherently weak'.[9] Capital works to establish and entrench inequalities that are destructive of solidarity and productive of competitive aggression and self-interest. Against this, he considers the historical culture of Chinese *Guanxi*, a fundamental and often tacit code that ensures social cohesion (Sennett, 2013, pp. 135–136). *Guanxi* tries to ensure connectedness among participants in a polity of any kind, and, citing Douglas Guthrie on it, Sennett writes that, under this code, 'You can count on other people in the network, especially when the going gets tough; they are honour-bound to support you rather than take advantage of your weakness' (Sennett, 2013, p. 135).

In this context, we can again call on the memory of Jimmy Reid's Glasgow Rectorial Address, on how a rat-race competition – especially if it is misapplied to institutions where it has no place, such as the university – can destroy the values proper to civil society. Instead, we find ourselves now in the position where we fear that criticism, dissent and even debate of any kind is unwelcome, even 'in the face of injustice', and why? The answer is 'lest you jeopardize your chances of promotion and self-advancement'. This is the opposite of responsible citizenship.

It might be worth considering this in terms of the contemporary demand, almost worldwide, for what in the United Kingdom is called 'widening participation': a determination to ensure that there is broader and better access among a society's citizenry to a university education such that our institutions do not constitute a finishing school and networking association for the elite or the 1% so astutely identified by Stiglitz, and so pointedly targeted by the Occupy movement. The 'widening participation' agenda is supposed to ensure that the strong do not take advantage of the inherent weakness of the underprivileged or poor; in principle, it is akin therefore to *Guanxi*.

Such a demand sounds moral and admirable, and, indeed, I am myself quite possibly a paradigmatic product of it. My own biography is that of a working-class east end of Glasgow childhood. I am the first in my family ever to remain in education beyond the age of 15. We did not own real estate: the house we lived in was owned by the City Council, and we paid rent for it. My father worked in the shipyards of the Clyde; my mother was a seamstress; both had left school at 14, and both had to work to sustain our existence. This was an unlikely background to produce a Professor of English and Comparative Literature.

---

[9] Richard Sennett, *Together* (Penguin, London, 2013), 134.

This is not to romanticize the story: the matter at issue is much more important than that. In the light of the story, what could be said – what, indeed, could I myself say – against the idea of widening participation, as an approach to securing my own contemporary kind of lifestyle for more working-class children? Well, it is worth remembering, for a start, that I was also the *only* child from my primary school who stayed on in education beyond 15, and that was from a class of over 40 in a school that had seven such classes. What happens to the other pupils, over 280 of them? Should our society be content with a less than 0.35% success rate in this matter? Does a 0.35% success rate in 'widening participation' justify a state of affairs where the rest – 99.65% – are denied opportunities for substantial and authoritative participation in the determination of the structure and values of their society?

We are often given a measure of how successful or otherwise our university sector has been in this activity of widening participation. A good example is that Oxford and Cambridge Universities sometimes find themselves castigated on the grounds that they fail in the widening participation agenda. For example, in the academic year 2009–2010, the figures show that they admitted only 40 students who came from a national constituency of some 80,000 who are so poor that they are provided with free school meals. This is, indeed, a disgrace, amounting to some 0.05% of such pupils. However, by castigating Oxford and Cambridge on this (which it remains justified to do), we forget that the real scandal is that the United Kingdom, which in recent years has varied in position as somewhere between the fourth and the eighth largest economy in the world, has some 80,000 schoolchildren who live in such abject poverty that they are eligible for free school meals. Would it therefore be somehow more acceptable if Oxford and Cambridge admitted, let's say, 100-times more than their current 40? That would still leave 76,000 such pupils. That – the structure of social inequality that has produced this number – is the real atrocity, and an attention on, say, my own individual luck, is a rather suave and elegant way of diverting attention from the failures of the political class to address such a damaging state of affairs. The romance replaces the reality, and the reality is one of unequal citizenship, unequal participation in a supposed 'democratic' society.

Similar figures are available for the Russell Group as a whole (the 2010–2011 cycle yielding the most recent data), and these show a fall year-on-year in the number of pupils from these poor backgrounds, and give the actual figure as (on average) 64 pupils per each institution (Cambridge admitting just 25, Oxford just 15). Nationally, in this period, 18% of 4- to 15-year-old pupils in the

United Kingdom qualified for free school meals.[10] Wendy Piatt, director general of the Russell Group, has repeatedly defended this position, blaming factors outside of the Russell Group or its admissions policies.

Where, we might ask, is the spirit of anything like *guanxi* to be found here? The figures bear an uncanny closeness to Stiglitz's identification of the relations between the 99% and the 1%, and the question to ask here is about the commitment of that 1% to itself, as against its commitment to the public life of citizenship as a whole.

This is a damaging state of affairs because it cannot reasonably be expected that these 80,000 or so individuals can 'participate' in a democratic franchise with any degree of real substance. 'Deny to working-class children any common share in the immaterial, and presently they will grow into the men who demand with menaces a communism of the material', wrote George Sampson in his *English for the English*. That was written in the wake of revolutionary fervour across Europe that Sampson and others feared after 1917. The shocking thing since that time is precisely that, notwithstanding some atrocious inequalities that structure our societies, there is, now, no such fear. The universities have played their part in 'normalizing' the value of mass inequalities of participation in the social formation.

There is no sense here that we are 'together' or that we form a 'citizenry of mutual responsibilities'; rather, we are divided – and not just by class. Perhaps more fundamentally, we are divided not just through unequal access to university and the education that it engages, but also by a profoundly unequal access to the social sphere, to politics and thus to citizenship – the life of the *politēs* – itself. The poor, very often, are not regarded properly as citizens at all; at best, they are an underclass of sorts, tacitly deemed to be not suitable for 'higher' education. They are like T.S. Eliot's 'young man carbuncular' in *The Waste Land*, the 'small house-agent's clerk …/One of the low on whom assurance sits/As a silk hat on a Bradford millionaire'. This, contemporaneous with Sampson above, indicates a culture's sense of social hierarchy or class, and the undesirability of social mobility. Yet, some social mobility must be tolerated if we are to avoid real social upheaval, and the way we tolerate it is by allowing a rare individual to be a scandalous and comically inappropriate figure: the man from Bradford who has succeeded in upwards financial mobility but whose fundamental biological and class vulgarity remains visible in his unsuitability for the trappings of his new class, the silk hat.

---

[10] See THE, 12 January 2014; see also David Willetts, written parliamentary answer to Peter Aldous, MP, written on 7 January 2014: Hansard: HC Deb, 7 January 2014, c191w.

Owen Jones, in his book, *Chavs*, records the history of the last half century (broadly from the mid-60s onwards) as a period during which the working-class has been systematically demonized. Further than this, he also demonstrates how it is that the working-class, especially *as a class*, have disappeared from any discussions about society: not only is it that 'class' is hardly ever explicitly mentioned by the political parties, but also the very recognition of a collective of people grouped according to their labour is no longer considered valid. This was dramatized through the 1980s in the Thatcher government's systematic attack upon trade unionism. Citizenship no longer extends to working-class people, to put this succinctly, and the cliché is that 'we are all middle-class' now, and therefore living together in a supposedly 'classless' society.

This differs from, say, the 1960s. At that time, the working-class existed as not just a cornerstone of society, but also as a respected community whose needs and values – like those of other citizens in other classes – had to be acknowledged, respected and addressed. This said, it was a class that was already under some pressures from the contemporary emergence of mass culture and its attendant armature of populist advertising. As Richard Hoggart showed in his classic *Uses of Literacy*, the working class had traditionally enjoyed great social cohesion and, through intrinsic ideals of social community, were able to resist the depredations of a capitalism, grounded in mass-cultural consumerism, that became eventually so rampant that even this solidarity came under strain.

Consider what has happened since then. Popular culture provides the perfect paradigmatic example. First, starting in the 1960s in popular musical culture, groups such as the Beatles are marketed as a kind of likeable 'cheeky-chappy' group, satirically getting above their working-class station and delighting people by their irreverence. When they played the 'Royal Variety Performance' show on 4 November 1963, before the UK's Royal Family, John Lennon famously introduced the closing song, 'Twist and Shout', by saying 'For our last number, I'd like to ask your help. Would the people in the cheaper seats clap your hands – and the rest of you, if you'd just rattle your jewellery ...' Interviewed prior to playing, he was told that he would probably have to watch his language and diction, as the then Conservative Prime Minister of the United Kingdom, Edward Heath, had said that he 'couldn't distinguish the words that the Beatles were singing', to which Lennon replied, in a satirically 'posh' voice, 'I don't understand Ted Heath; I don't understand Teddy saying that at all, really,' and, after a pause, adding, much more seriously and in his own non-metropolitan Liverpool accent, 'We're not going to vote for Ted'.

It would take many years before Lennon came to write a song such as 'Working-Class Hero', in 1970, in which the dark seriousness of the class issue that lay behind the light irreverence of 1963 would come more to the fore. One key aspect of that 1970 song is precisely a warranted cynicism about the ways in which we now understand 'widening participation', for much of the song's anger and even self-disgust is directed precisely at the ways in which the working-class hero is accommodated by and co-opted by the middle classes. While Lennon himself returned his MBE in 1969 as a gesture of political protest against war in Biafra and Vietnam, and while he supported Jimmy Reid by contributing financially to the Upper Clyde Shipbuilders in their work-in in 1971, his former fellow-Beatle, Paul McCartney, was knighted in 1997. Indeed, Mick Jagger of the Rolling Stones, who through the 1960s and since were marketed as the more 'dangerous' or subversive and anti-establishment band, notwithstanding Jagger's own personal rather more middle-class background, was himself knighted in 2003.

In those earlier days, then, the working class were moving from first of all being respected as a class to becoming the subject – and then gradually the object – of comedy. This is the story of the Beatles, with their irreverent humour, and the self-conscious zaniness of their comic films. Second, however, the 'danger' that the class represented, considered *as a class*, becomes 'contained' in the controllable figure of the great rival group, the Stones, from whose dark satanic image, associated especially with Keith Richards (to be later 'domesticated', as noted earlier, in Johnny Depp's pirate-character), would then proceed an entire so-called underground culture.

Within the decade, however, these were all becoming invisible, as we 'all' became middle-class: the underground becomes a 'progressive' and intellectualized rock music; Pink Floyd share a concert platform with Stockhausen; Emerson, Lake and Palmer play Mussorgsky; Yes open their live concerts with Stravinsky's 'Firebird'. Thus opens that clichéd idea of the 'postmodern' as the supposed breaking-down of barriers between high and low culture. But behind that cliché lie these serious class issues, and these are related fundamentally to what is also happening in universities. Sex and drugs and Rock-and-roll were initially emblematic of a so-called 'counterculture', itself associated with the intellectuals and earlier Beatniks; but, by the time that Ian Dury and the Blockheads sang of them in 1977, the very idea of such a counterculture has been thoroughly tamed. It is no longer something to fear, but something to be treated lightly, even celebrated. By the time the Sex Pistols sang 'God save the Queen ... and the Fascist regime' in 1977, they might have been doing just that. Alwyn Turner points out that this song was supposedly counter-establishment in 1977, when the Queen celebrated her Silver Jubilee; but that 'it also ... tied the group so closely to the institution of monarchy they were attacking that come the Golden Jubilee in 2002, they seized the marketing opportunity with glee, playing reunion gigs and releasing a three-CD box set. The long-known ability of the British establishment to assimilate and neutralize its critics was evidently still intact.'[11]

This detour into popular music may seem to be of peripheral interest; however, it is important to note that these turns in popular culture all coincided with the period of mass expansion of the UK university system following the 1963 Robbins Report. The parallel is that working-class children, the underprivileged, were being 'entertained' and accommodated as possible members of the elite, and the idea – ostensibly admirable if one subscribes to some intrinsic value of 'aspiration' – is that more working-class people will actually lose their affiliation to the working class, as if it is not acceptable to identify with that class any more. 'Aspiration' is the word used to cover an implicit denigration of working-class people, as if to be of this class is so undesirable that any sane or educated person will aspire to leave it. The idea, essentially, is – by design or by accident – to shrink the working class as a social group, and to do this by dividing the working class in terms of relative 'merit' or 'aspiration' or – worst of all – some sense of an intrinsic 'talent'. It is as if the 'talented' academically are all somehow at least secretly middle-class, and that some innate intelligence just has to be given the opportunity to break through the force of circumstance that had previously and somehow erroneously consigned them to working-class poverty. From this, we derive the idea of the middle class and upper class as somehow being intrinsically more intelligent than working-class people.

This is also, of course, the period when we see a flowering in literature of the 'campus novel', from Mary McCarthy's 1951 *Groves of Academe* in the United States, mutating very quickly into the ideologically very different United Kingdom texts, such as Kingsley Amis's *Lucky Jim* (1954) which deals explicitly with class mobility, and then on to the 1970s and 1980s texts of David Lodge and Malcolm Bradbury. The texts of these last two embody fully the peculiar attempt to regulate the comic demands of a satire on universities with the tragic effects (divorce, even death in the case of Bradbury's *The History Man*, probably the most celebrated of these texts) that are brought about by social, pedagogical and cultural tensions.

The mania for examining children academically at earlier and earlier ages – the most egregious example of which is perhaps the British '11-plus' exam, an examination used even to the present day as a way of determining which children are worthy of on-going academic education – is worth considering. Among the middle classes, it operates as what we might call 'the Mozart syndrome'. Mozart, famously, was a child prodigy, and, in our time, we see endless anxieties – thanks

---

[11] Alwyn Turner, *Crisis? What Crisis?* (Aurum Press, London, 2008; reproduced 2013), 162.

to the testing and examining regime that scars our schools – about whether our children have reached certain extraordinary standards of academic proficiency at ages as young as three or four. Behind this, however, lies a much darker thought: if, indeed, academic 'talent' is so apparent at these earlier and earlier ages, then, in the final analysis, it must somehow be 'inherent' in some children, lying there latent even before they are born. It is, as it were, 'inherited', genetically. Class becomes equated with eugenics, and both with wealth. If this is so, then why do we need universities – indeed, why bother with schools – at all?

Following from this we see the emergence of private and for-profit institutions, given the state's (by now ostensibly 'logical') withdrawal of financial interest in the relation between education and citizenship. Education, by this point, has become a way of 'gaming' – or gambling – in a society where the odds are already well stacked, and profiteers step in at this moment to make their money out of 'aspiration'. The for-profiteers operate on principles similar to those governing national lotteries. However, whereas national lotteries encourage gambling, largely by poorer people, on the basis that 'it could be you' who wins, by contrast the 'for-profiteers' adopt the same principle, but based on the 'it *should* be you', the advertising slogan that justifies extravagant spending 'because I'm worth it'.

Now, after decades of the cynical co-opting of working-class people and values, the ideological norm suggests that if you are poor, then it is due to your lack of merit or your lack of aspiration or, worst of all, your genes and biological inheritance. As a result, you are not fully a member of our civic polity: lacking merit, you are worth less than others; lacking aspiration, your lack of worth is your own fault. This is straightforward disenfranchisement, and no amount of pious words about 'widening participation' will address the fundamental issues at stake. Those issues are to do with the relation of democracy to citizenship, and at the core of this is the instrument of education and especially of university education, seen as a door to wealth, personal riches, self-aggrandizement and the satisfaction of the appropriate aspirations.

3.6 BUREAUCRACY, OR THE END OF CIVILITY IN THE UNIVERSITY

This is all a rather bleak, even disastrous, picture. The trouble is that it is borne out by evidence, and that it actually is not at all polemical. Can we counter this? What is a better role for the university in relation to these issues?

Given our focus on citizenship, we could make a positive turn by considering a 'social contract', in the style of Rousseau, say, or an extension of Sennett's *guanxi*. However, my case here is that this is itself rather too limited for a proper consideration of the relation of the citizen to the secular or worldly institution. A better way of thinking of things, following especially from the economic considerations in this chapter and in my previous chapter on 'duty', is to think in terms of a 'social debt', a kind of duty owed to the social itself. The citizen, I shall contend, is she or he who engages the social precisely as a kind of duty, and who sees that duty as itself being constitutive of our being together in a public or commons.

This duty or social debt is itself characterized by the modes of connection and contact that hold the public together, or that establish the public in terms of a commonly shared constitutional citizenship. It should be noted that this is entirely and fundamentally at odds with the prevailing norms that govern how we think of the functioning of our universities. Those norms treat of the university, and indeed of the social itself, as a kind of arithmetical agglomeration or accretion of discrete and atomized individuals. The university is, in this view, at best an *agora* or *forum* to which previously entirely unrelated individuals come, engage as if in a market or commercial enterprise in the seeking of personal gain and then leave again, returning once more to their prior identity, changed only to the extent that they are commercially or wealthily enhanced by the university as market, shopping mall and gambling den. We might consider restoring the idea of the *collegium* against this.

We should start from the real conditions of people. We do not come, Robinson Crusoe like, from deserted islands into a market of relative exploit and exploitation; rather, we were always already a constituent part of the society that established the very possibility of there being a *forum* or *agora* in the first place. That public thing, that *res publica*, is there entirely because of our previously existing social relations, our being-together. Instead of arithmetic, think geometry – literally the measuring of the earth and its constructed shape as an intrinsic and integrated whole.

In thinking 'geometrically', we can reassert the centrality of those questions of force with which we began. In some ways, the consideration of force that I outlined earlier – force of nature and force of circumstance – is a re-elaboration of Hobbes. Famously, in *Leviathan*, Hobbes found the social condition to be a continual war of all against all, with the result that life is 'nasty, brutish and short'. To contest this, Hobbes argues that individuals sublimate their natural force, as it were, looking to some higher and shared good, and the generalized subscription to that higher force (a force of political circumstance, essentially) counters the negativity of natural violence. In modern poetry, the equivalent is to be found in Charles Olson, for whom 'projective geometry' helped explain how objects in the world *made space* for themselves, but for themselves as things-in-relation-to-others.[12]

---

[12] I am grateful to David Herd for drawing this parallel to my attention. In this, Olson establishes poetry as an emanation of breathing, in which 'it comes to this: culture displacing the state'. Culture, in this, re-establishes out mutual intimacies.

In some ways, this is a succinct defence of what we might now call 'public goods' arguments that I will place at the centre of the university as an institution engaged with citizenship. The very sustainability of life – our capacity for survival – is consequent upon a *collective* act, which calls us into a series of mutual duties or debts to each other, debts whose existence produces the tensions and glues that hold the social together as a dynamic geometrical frame. The frame requires regulation, and it is this that we sometimes call collaboration, and sometimes call competition. In both cases, however, the prior existence of our contact with each other, our connectedness together, is a necessary given. It follows from this that a university should axiomatically be concerned with citizenship, and that such citizenship accepts collective – if always fluid and dynamic – identities, while rejecting the idea of the atomized individual coming to market and returning individually enriched, even at the cost of others.

This structure or foundation for citizenship is, however, precisely the thing that has been under attack now for some decades by a neo-liberal economic dogma that has been either systematically forced upon the university sector or, in some cases, warmly embraced by some in the established but oligarchical leadership of that sector. The rapid development and 'normalization' of that dogma is seen most clearly in the United Kingdom, where the Browne Review famously rejected the idea of the university education as having anything to do with the public good, seeing it instead primarily – even purely at times – as an instrument of private gain. It is for this reason, among many others, that the Browne Review not only betrays the very idea of a university, but also constitutes an attack upon connected citizenship and upon the *collegium* as a model of the university.

For Sennett, civility grows out of earlier social norms governed by the logic of 'courtesy', the rituals of the court. He relates this to Castiglione, for whom the development of such civility required what he called *sprezzatura*, a kind of lightness of spirit. 'In Castiglione's view, lightness made people more "companionable", that is, more cooperative in conversation. Less self, more sociable' (Sennett, p. 117). That aphoristic final phrase – less self, more sociable – cuts close to the nub of my case here that the self depends upon prior companionship. The very possibility of human individuation derives from the fact of our being already enmeshed socially – in civic partnership and collegiality – with each other. We do not 'come together' as an arithmetical addition of bodies; we are always together in the first place. The *collegium* is, as it were, our actual and natural condition.

Interestingly in relation to Chapter 1, Sennett points out that the resulting civility here is grounded in what he calls the deployment of 'minimum force' in our relations with each other and with our environment. He relates his argument about togetherness back to his earlier work on *The Craftsman*, where he laid out the conditions of skill as a form of 'embodied knowledge'. In *Together*, he explains this in terms of the development of sensitivity in, for example, the way a surgeon learns the skill of using a scalpel, or the way a luthier learns the skill of making a cello from wood that may be roughened by knots.

In considering the craftsman – luthier or surgeon, say – at work, he argues that their hand necessarily meets resistance of various kinds, be it in the wood to be carved or the skin, tissue or organs to be cut. He argues that 'Applying minimum force is the most effective way to work with resistance', because 'the less aggressive the effort, the greater the sensitivity' (Sennett, p. 210), vital in the case of surgery. However, he goes on to extend this, and not just as metaphor, into the realm of our social engagement as well. This, in short, explains the development of international diplomacy or, at the micro-level, fundamental social relations. These, he says, are properly conditioned by 'restraint'. His case is that, as with the learning of a skill as something that accommodates the relation between our hands, say, and the environment, so also we have 'embodied social knowledge' (Sennett, p. 211). This, he argues, is fundamental to our being. He writes that 'in deploying minimum force, both physically and socially, we can become more sensitive to, more connected with, more engaged by the environment. The things or people that resist our will, the experiences which resist our instant understanding, can come to matter in themselves' (Sennett, p. 212).

This, in some ways, is also a fine description of the activity of learning itself. Importantly, once again, physical force is seen as something that needs to be regulated as a condition of such learning, and this requires our literal 'collegiality', and requires that we craft such collaboration with sensitivity, to counter the 'natural' force of the bully or 'master' who revels in unearned authority over us.

With this, we dispense immediately with any idea of the university conditioned by MOOCs. The MOOC is grounded fundamentally in an atomized social conditioning: it is anathema to the condition of a university, and it constitutes also a threat to the civilizing power of learning, which must axiomatically be a collective activity, carried out as a public good and serving the geometry of our world, environment or social relatedness. In this respect, the virtual public realm is not the realm of citizenship. Further, in the evisceration of citizenship from the public realm, this move into the virtual also reduces the civilizing activity of 'knowing' to the status of mere 'information transfer'.

Knowing requires interaction, and requires the reintroduction of *doubt*, that is, the civilizing condition of 'restraint'. The realm of the univocal, in which knowledge presents no problems or doubt because we now have the requisite correct information, is the realm of tyranny, not citizenship. Tyranny works by force; citizenship by restraint occasioned by doubt and by the consequent duty we have to each other to remain in relatedness, in collegiality. Doubt is a measure of our commitment to dialogue, and thus to community, and citizenship is now measured by our debt to such social relation as the very condition of the possibility of our individuality.

Sennett also alludes to Norbert Elias's work on *The Civilizing Process*, where Elias demonstrated how civility grows with bodily restraint. At one extreme, this meant that it became unacceptable to fart in public, or to ensure the delicacy of the knife and fork mediating relations between living hand and bloody meat; at another extreme, it disallows rape and encourages the rituals and deferring pleasures and sociability of courtship. For Elias, this further relates to a psychology of shame, and its consequences in politics. There is, in civility, a pressing need for shame: shame, in some ways, is what determines the requirement for restraint and for minimum force. And, as Elias points out, there are large political consequences here. One necessary partial explanation for the enormous atrocity of the Nazis is that the Nazis knew no shame, and that consequently there was nothing to restrain what Sennett calls 'their inner beast'.

Citizenship is antithetical to such violence and to the covert coercion that drives relentlessly towards the demands for conformity. One way of tacitly endorsing conformity and disallowing or de-legitimizing dissent, of course, is through bureaucratic protocols: the establishment of 'standard' processes, whose 'value' is simply contained in the 'validity' of their execution, not in any material content. The university, therefore, should realize the shame of such tyranny and should reclaim itself as the site or event that we celebrate as dissent, the unorthodox, 'things undreamt of in our philosophies', the calling back into doubt of 'the standard', and above all calling into question the modes of standardization that are the consequence of the triumph of bureaucracy.

In that 1972 Rectorial Address to which I have already referred, Jimmy Reid also considered the changing living conditions of working-class people, as housing estates gave way to massive tower blocks. He noted the way in which such housing atomized and segregated individuals, such that civic community itself was threatened. Yet more pointedly, however, he asked us to note the visual similarity between the tower block and the tall filing cabinet of modern bureaucratic life. As in other totalitarian or authoritarian societies, human individuals were now in danger of becoming reference numbers, their lives governed by 'standardization', and 'contained' in a file, marked by abstract headings that were not of their own choosing, and subject to the organization by others of their conditions. The result of this is a drive towards standardization that mutates very easily into a drive towards conformity, and which, in turn, mutates very quickly into a drive towards homogeneity and the eradication of the heterogeneous, the unorthodox, the dissenting and even individuation itself.

The current trend for quantification of quality in the sector should therefore be reversed. The consequence of this is that bureaucratic process – when it becomes a replacement for content – should be challenged. The difficulty, however, lies in the tyranny of number, an abstract entity of measurement that substitutes measure itself for truth. There is a relevant history to this for our purposes here, and it starts at the time of the First Great Crash and Recession.

In 1932, the economist and businessman Alfred Cowles stopped making stock market forecasts, having become convinced, after the 1929 crash, that forecasting was really nothing more sophisticated than guesswork: gambling blind, as it were. He decided that he needed to undertake some solid research before returning to the investment market, and so he opened his Commission for Research in Economics in Colorado Springs. The Commission's motto, retained in Chicago where it became a Foundation, was initially 'Science is measurement'. Econometrics would yield investment certainty.

The idea that measurement brings investment certainty persists in our day. One example is the number of contact-hours a student has with teachers in the new dispensation in which a university education is cast as a quasi-privatized investment. Contact is important; but the quantifying of hours occludes the more serious issues: *quality* of contact, and what we want from it. The logic of university learning is that students, through the very activity of their study, develop autonomy and establish independent authority as they inaugurate their futures. Such a logic implies that students need progressively fewer contact-hours as they progress, as reliance on the teacher's authority cedes place to their own emergent autonomy. However, the econometric market-logic requires quantification of the investment and presses the student to argue for *increases* in contact-hours, thereby *compromising their education*. Market-logic endangers the very point of higher education.

Quantifying hours leads only to guesswork ('how much is enough?': should it be 8 per week; or 12; maybe 15; how about 20?), and the result is *always* unsatisfactory, for the number becomes an inadequate proxy for the more pressing question of how well a student is *integrated* with the discipline, with the collegium or university institution, and with her or his peers. The measuring and quantifying of 'contact-hours' becomes a *substitute* for actual engagement and for the qualitative activity of knowing which, as I have argued above, is itself conditioned by the maintenance of doubt and the consequent requirement for more communal or collective dialogue – research, in short.

Here is another motto: 'only connect'. In his 1910 novel, *Howards End*, E.M. Forster makes a plea for a kind of integrated life-experience, where, as he puts it, passion is connected to prose, the spirited life of the body to the cool life of the mind, impassioned intellect to hard-headed business and realpolitik. Against this are the forces of fragmentation, forces that atomize societies into discrete individuals constructing lives as a series of accountable business transactions. The contact-hours fetish is simply one symptom of that atomized society, and of the ongoing commodification of 'knowledge' itself. Such an attitude has no place in any university education worthy of the name, for it implies that once the contact is over, so also is the education. The *quality* of our connectedness – of our education, of our society – is properly revealed instead by our students' growing autonomy and authority, and if good, that is immeasurable, unaccountable.

We live, it will be said, in the most 'connected' societies ever. Phenomena such as texting, tweeting, Facebook, Instagram, tumblr and a host of other social media sites have ensured that we all appear to be constantly online for a relatedness from which there is no escape, as if we have taken fully to heart the injunction to 'only connect'. Indeed, when we are all now as teachers enjoined to deploy every aspect of contemporary technology, it won't be long before lectures themselves develop into 'interactive' tweeted 'discussion'. This has consequences for our interest in contact-hours. If I take time to text during a lecture, should I subtract those minutes when I account for my contact-time? What if the text that I send or receive relates to the matter in hand? In the interests of market econometrics, we are in danger of becoming increasingly, pointlessly, Jesuitical about figures.

The real question relates instead to the material engagements between teachers and learners, and to the quality of their integration with each other in the pursuit of knowledge relevant to the discipline. We could call it 'teaching-led research'. It involves not just contact between teacher and student; but contact between both of them and the future of their discipline: we teach to learn what our students will become. This, too, is civic, civilizing, citizenship.

The motto 'science is measurement' derives from an 1879 painting by Henry Stacy Marks. It shows the scientist, armed with a measuring tape, before the skeleton of a pelican. The irony is clear: reduced to measurement, science kills. The current obsession with quantified hours – and to the more general substitution of bureaucratic validation as a replacement for the value of material content in our mutual and collegial activities – leads to the fragmentation deplored by Forster. It is consistent with the atomization of social and university life into the activities of discrete individuals, isolated in the market-place. Such atomization guarantees only unhappiness. The university, however, is not a market-place where individuals come to account for or to buy time; it is precisely a mode of being together, of seeking communities and forging shared futures, and these are immune from measurement, but open to questions of quality. That is the point of contact: connectedness with each other, and not mere econometric clock-watching. Even the Cowles Foundation, now at Yale, no longer believes that science is measurement. Nor should we.

The university, as an entity that conditions the possibility of citizenship, should therefore reclaim the fundamental value of the collegium, and of the diplomacy that, perhaps paradoxically, encourages dissent in the interests of establishing a commonality of the pursuit of knowing.

4
OF GOVERNANCE AND GOVERNMENT

> Of all people, academics ought to have a professional interest in unconstrained intellectual freedom ... Every time you go into your workplace, you leave a democracy behind and enter a dictatorship. Nowhere else is freedom of speech for the citizens of free societies so curtailed ... If employees criticize their employers in public ...they will face a punishment as hard as a prison sentence, maybe harder: the loss of their career, their pension, and perhaps their means of making a livelihood.
>
> (Nick Cohen, *You Can't Read This Book*, 79; pp. 149–150)

4.1 GOVERNING ONE'S TONGUE

University governance and political government are related. The way in which our university institutions are governed (governance) works intimately and intricately in conjunction with the political modes shaping how the society is governed (government). And, in recent times, the thing that has to be governed, above all, is the tongue. 'Govern your tongue'; 'whatever you say, say nothing'; 'be diplomatic'; work 'behind the scenes' (which is, of course, what corruption encourages and what encourages corruption) – these are all examples of what has become a key aspect of both government and governance in recent times.

A brief consideration of shifts in political and government manoeuvring over the last quarter century or so will help clarify, with the United Kingdom as a paradigmatic example. When Labour lost power in 1979, it went not only into opposition, but also into ideological turmoil. Throughout the 1980s, the Party became difficult to control, and it split into various contestatory ideological groupings or 'factions'. The perception among the electorate that the Party was at civil war with itself contributed to its remaining out of power for 18 years. Although the ideological Left got the blame for this, it was in fact a group of individuals from the ideological Right of the Party who did, in fact, break the Party up: Roy Jenkins, Shirley Williams, David Owen and Bill Rogers broke away and formed the SDP or Social Democratic Party. It became apparent to one MP who had entered parliament in 1983, Tony Blair, that factionalism such as this would guarantee permanent opposition and no hope of gaining governmental power.

Similarly, through the later 1980s and into the 1990s, the Conservative Party also started to fall into similar dysfunction. To the annoyance of many in the Party, Thatcher was deposed and replaced by John Major. He, too, had enormous difficulty in reining in the contestatory elements within the Conservatives, and here, the most frequent focus for dysfunction was the question of immigration, which was hidden under debates about 'Europe' and British identity. The immigration issue was a long-lasting legacy of Enoch Powell's famous 'rivers of blood' speech, made in Wolverhampton in 1974, through which a vein of xenophobia within the Party had been opened, haemorrhaging for long enough eventually to bleed into the formation of an entirely new party, the UK Independence Party. Along the way, the Right had also been tarnished by the proximity of its positions on immigration with the more openly racist policies of far-Right parties such as the British Nationalist Party and, later, English Defence League. 'Europe' allowed these issues to be played out more safely than any openly racist arguments; but, although the pro- and anti-European factions thus avoided the censure of the electorate, they nonetheless showed that the Conservatives, like Labour in the 1980s, were at open war with themselves.

Both major political parties realized that, if they were to gain and keep governmental power, there had to be a strict rein on anything that threatened a sense of unity. This was dealt with through two things: essentially a 'rebranding' exercise, in which the Labour Party became 'New Labour', and the rise to centrality of the role of the spin doctor. The key task of the political spin doctor was, as the very name suggests, to keep matters in a healthy condition through turning stories that might be negative into positive goods. As Milton's Satan has it in *Paradise Lost* – albeit in what might look like an extreme formulation – 'Evil, be thou my good'. Or, as Peter Mandelson had it, in a formulation that is equally frightening if rather less dramatically stated, the spin doctor's task is 'to create the truth'.[1]

The manipulation of language, such that things might appear to be their very opposites, becomes key. However, that is not enough: all members of the Party now have to ensure unity by toeing the line on this. It is a situation brilliantly satirized in the figure of Malcolm Tucker, in Armando Ianucci's film, *In the Loop* (2009). The film opens with spin doctor Malcolm Tucker (played by Peter Capaldi) being handed the usual day's 'monitoring': discs with recordings of MP media appearances. The first disc he plays is a recording of a hapless Minister of International Development, Simon Foster (played by Tom Hollander), ambushed in a radio interview, saying that a US-led war in the Middle East is 'unforeseeable'. Tucker flies into a rage, and immediately starts phoning newspapers, which have picked up on the 'war is unforeseeable' statement: 'You may have *heard* him say that, but he did *not* say that … And that's a fact'. When Tucker finds Foster in his office, he barks at him that 'That's not the line. Walk the fucking line'.

This lays bare what is at issue: there is an official line, determined by the spin doctor, and all members of the party have to walk that line. There is, in effect, a centralization of power within the party itself, which requires conformity among all members. There can be no dissent, no dialogue and no debate: just follow the line, like a stage-actor taking direction and rehearsing lines written by another author. The very authority of the individual MP is thus constrained. JFK's famous 'Think not what your country can do for you' aphorism is shortened, to 'Think not'.[2]

In the university sector, we see internal governance following precisely the same prescription. First, there is the gradual but accumulative introduction of the 'brand', which requires presentational unity: the acquisition of a logo, the development of a marketable strapline for all official paperwork, all headed notepaper carrying logo and strapline, the production of branded merchandise, from tee shirts to pencils, with higher-end materials such as jewellery or expensive artefacts whose exclusivity by price matches the university's exclusivity by prestige, and so on. Branding requires not just uniforms and uniformity, but also conformity: those who carry the brand – that is, the academic and

---

[1] Alwyn Turner, *A Classless Society* (Aurum Books, London, 2013), 334.

[2] In relation to this, see also Henry A. Giroux, 'Thinking dangerously in an age of political betrayal', available at: http://www.truthdig.com/report/item/thinking_dangerously_in_an_age_of_political_betrayal_20140718.

student bodies, as well as the administrators – are expected to 'walk the line'. If they do not, they risk being placed in a position where the university authorities can jeopardize their careers by suggesting that their non-conformist statements threaten the brand, thereby menacing the standing and standardization of the university's reputation, and thus 'bringing the university into disrepute'.[3]

No university has ever adopted the appropriate strapline, which would be something like: 'Here, we disagree about everything, and we resolve those disagreements by a process of argument and debate, trial and very important error, which we see as fundamental to good research and teaching'. While conformity might be appropriate for a political party seeking election to government, it is completely opposite to the essential duties of a university. It is this – the modelling of universities along brand-lines like political parties – that represented the real and fundamental politicization of the sector, and it is this politicization that has led the sector into debility. The internalization of brand-loyalty, to replace loyalty to one's discipline and fidelity to the cause of dissent, argument, research, teaching and learning, all finds its ground in changes to the mode of internal governance.

Next, there is the rapid demise of senatorial dialogue and debate, as power is centralized in the hands of the few at the centre of management. Governance reviews (such as those in the United Kingdom led by Ron Dearing in 1997, and by Richard Lambert in 2003) lead, first of all, to reductions in the size of governing bodies (Councils), and to the insistence on there being a lay majority among those members of council. Lay members, while certainly very knowledgeable in many cases about the world of commerce or business outside the university, cannot be expected to know intimately the internal work of the institution itself. The consequence is that the VC effectively has control over the very council to which she or he is supposed to be answerable, since the VC can 'inform' the council with respect to any queries they may have regarding internal university affairs. The democratic powers of senates are reduced, as their constitution also becomes less 'representative' of academic or departmental and disciplinary interests. Instead of departments

---

[3] David Browne, a senior associate at the law firm SGH Martineau, caused controversy in July 2014, when he argued in his blog that universities might have to sack high-performing academics who had 'outspoken opinions', on the grounds that outspoken opinion damages the university brand. The resulting twitter-storm attracted much indignation, but one key point, surely, is that Browne's own 'outspoken opinion' here had itself damaged the SGH Martineau brand. Logically, therefore, he should sack himself. The position he defends, essentially, is authoritarianism and conformity: speak out, by all means, as long as you express or endorse the view of the boss thereby. For such yes-man argument, see: http://www.sghmartineau.com/Pressrelitem.aspx?CID=806#.U80ccFavvHg.

feeding their thoughts upwards in a university hierarchy, via senate representation, we have instead the VC handing directives downwards, but claiming legitimacy for those directives by 'sharing' them, passing them through a non-representative senate.

So, where government has spin doctors, universities have 'communications' officers; where political parties have whips, universities have brand-managers. In the university sector, both these functions are governed by the overarching control of what used to be called 'staff offices', or 'personnel offices' – but even these are now rebranded as 'human resources', or HR. HR officials now act, essentially, as the ultimate arbiters of conduct. HR has become something like the unofficial police force of the institutions, charged with ensuring 'best practices' across a 'suite' of activities and everyday engagements between and among academics, students and institutional power.

Finally, we should note one final correspondence between recent political practice and university governance: the demise of the status of 'experience' and especially of 'real-world experience'. Since at least 1997 in the United Kingdom, with the triumph of Tony Blair's rebranded New Labour in the election of that year, an emphasis has increasingly been placed on the value of the Party leader who is not just media-friendly (i.e. considered to be physically attractive in some way), but also on her or his youth. When Robin Cook was suggested as a contender for Labour party leadership, he was frank as to the reason for refusing to stand, saying that he looked 'too ugly' (Turner, p. 107). Blair was 44 when he came to power; David Cameron was 43; George Osborne was chancellor at 38. Few leading politicians among the major parties of our day have come into politics from other walks of life. Many, if not most, are PPE graduates, often from Oxbridge, who go into parliament as junior researchers or assistants (sometimes as unpaid interns), and, from this, provided they show themselves to be good apparatchiks, they proceed through internal ranks and eventually to safe seats in constituencies with which they have no geographical or biographical affiliations.

The key thing about this is that it essentially disqualifies the value of 'experience' and of worldly experience beyond the charmed circle of official politics. This should be aligned also with the rise of HR. HR officers take a necessarily generic approach to employment issues. That is the meaning of 'best practice': only by comparing practices that are different according to their different and particular situations can one compare best and worst, and only by then reducing these to whatever they have as a lowest possible common denominator, can one find something applicable to all. 'HR professionals' can move from banking to heavy industry to university to hospitals and so on – without experience or even proper understanding of how these institutions best operate. Paradoxically, therefore, 'best practice' requires the deterioration of attention to the specifics of actual lived experience, and the reduction of actuality to an abstraction that has no contact with empirical realities.

It follows that 'best practice', in the field of HR, is actually the worst practice of all. The result of that is that HR has to reduce the content of any specific employment issue to zero, or to the lowest possible common denominator, so that a supposed parity of treatment – a bogus 'democratic equality' – across all sorts of different activity can be monitored and ensured. It is consistent with what Chris Dillow has described as one of the many problems of 'managerialist ideology – the belief that all organizations can be managed from above by leaders'.[4]

One senior HR official once referred to me as 'the professorial function in the English department'. This is typical of a specific kind of mechanistic thinking: the institution, for this kind of HR, is a machine with different functions (or, probably, 'functionalities' as the jargon would put it, since unnecessarily lengthened words sound more authoritativistic in the realmicity of manageriology). The task is simply to keep the machine running. We have known of this for some time, in fact: it is at the core of Charlie Chaplin's great critical satire in *Modern Times*, in which he becomes precisely a cog in a machine. It is not a huge move from this to the parodic situation of the character of Jen in Graham Linehan's much more recent television sitcom, *The IT Crowd*. Jen knows absolutely nothing about IT, cannot operate the 'on' switch for her computer and spends entire days doing nothing except staring at her desk. Her role in Renholm Industries is 'Relationship Manager'; many universities now have our own version of Jen: senior HR colleagues in roles with titles such as 'Employee Relations Manager', 'Rewards Manager', 'Job Evaluation Manager', and the like with similar titles (for each 'Manager' there is also usually a corresponding Director, Assistant, Deputy Assistant and so on, in an obese bloating of office). The great paradox is that HR is the realm of the non-job job.

Many senior HR individuals come to the university from the private and commercial sectors, and they import practices from the commercial sector directly into the university's management systems that are entirely inappropriate and, indeed, contrary to the very spirit and idea of a collegium. A simple example is 'line management': in this, a hierarchy is established, pushing power upwards and responsibility downwards. Essentially, the further up one goes, the more

---

[4] Chris Dillow blogs at: http://stumblingandmumbling.typepad.com/stumbling_and_mumbling/2007/04/managerialism_p.html.

power and less actual responsibility one has, while, inversely, the more junior one is, the more responsibility but less actual power one has. Another way of describing 'line management' structures is simply 'the delegation of blame'. At the top of the line in the hierarchy, one never finds any individual who accepts responsibility for things going wrong: if they go wrong, it is the managerial system that is at fault, not the senior managers who have invented it, endorsed it and who operate it. By contrast, at the bottom of the line, responsibility is total and power non-existent. Interestingly, however, if something goes well, the 'Rewards Manager' and the 'Remuneration Committee' suddenly find that this is all because of the individuals at the top of the line, who get their excessive pay rise. In this instance, those at the bottom who have actually done the successful hands-on work get the crumbs, if any are left. HR calls this 'incentivization'.

Such modes of management might also help explain the conundrum posed by Stefan Collini when he considers the importation of private sector norms into the university or other public institutions. Writing in the *LRB*, Collini says:

> Future historians, pondering changes in British society from the 1980s onwards, will struggle to account for the following curious fact. Although British business enterprises have an extremely mixed record (frequently posting gigantic losses, mostly failing to match overseas competitors, scarcely benefiting the weaker groups in society), and although such arm's length public institutions as museums and galleries, the BBC and the universities have by and large a very good record (universally acknowledged creativity, streets ahead of most of their international peers, positive forces for human development and social cohesion), nonetheless over the past three decades politicians have repeatedly attempted to force the second set of institutions to change so that they more closely resemble the first. Some of those historians may even wonder why at the time there was so little concerted protest at this deeply implausible programme. But they will at least record that, alongside its many other achievements, the coalition government took the decisive steps in helping to turn some first-rate universities into third-rate companies.[5]

Key to this situation has been the rise to centrality of HR, its reduction of individual academics and students to functioning elements in a machine (the professorial function; with, presumably, students as 'learning functions', working in 'learning-interaction environmental functions' – formerly known as 'seminars'), and the consequent systemic mistrust of dialogue or debate, even among colleagues. It is not simply that one must not answer back to one's superiors in the chain of line management. It is much, much, worse than that.

---

[5] Stefan Collini, 'Sold Out', *London Review of Books* 35: 20 (24 October 2013), 12.

In the service of a falsely constituted 'parity' of treatment (which is actually a reduction of humans to their lowest common abstract denominators, as 'functions' or 'resources'), HR atomizes the academy into constituent individualized elements, or parts. Our task is simply to be a function, a resource, and resources don't talk to each other, while functions do as they are told or instructed to do – or else they are declared 'broken' and need to be 'fixed' or thrown out and replaced.

For HR, everyone is replaceable; no one is unique, because experience is irrelevant to anything. This is so even in institutions that claim that their teaching is 'research-led'. Yet, if a colleague is, for example, 'suspended', then, mysteriously, another colleague whose research does not match that of the first's can nonetheless carry on with the excellent 'research-led teaching'. Collini criticizes the tendency within the modern institution to think of the university as a 'widget-factory' in an outmoded 19th-century industrial production model. What this really means is that students and academic staff are themselves the widgets in question.

It is for this reason that HR has driven us steadily towards the prioritization of processes, procedures and protocols over other important issues of actual content or actual events and workplace situations. It is also this, of course, that has led to the situation where it is increasingly felt that VCs no longer need any prior academic experience themselves. After all, they are now in many cases self-styled CEOs (implying the university is a straightforward commercial business enterprise); or they become self-styled 'presidents', with a corresponding sense of self-aggrandizement – but, crucially and unlike political presidents, *not elected*, and therefore essentially involved in a kind of institutional 'permanent *coup d'état*', in the memorable phrase that François Mitterrand coined to describe the way that General de Gaulle arrogated all power to himself.

The key thing that links government to governance, then, is a combination of 'governing one's tongue' to ensure conformity with the branded line, and a corresponding reduction in free speech or democratic participation.

What is at stake is nothing less than the democratic participation in the work of a society or of an institution. In short, democracy is replaced by two entirely different political orders: oligarchy (which we might now understand as 'rule by and for the elite' or by the 'presiding 1%') and bureaucracy, which Hannah Arendt described presciently in 1958 as 'rule by no-one', where matters of individual conscience and judgement are referred instead to an allegedly neutral 'system' of management. In this state of affairs, not only are people deprived of their legitimate voice (a word that is etymologically cognate with 'vote', as Coriolanus well knew), but also, extremely disturbingly, the expression of those voices – in a mode of dissent – is too often being met with force and violence, exerted in the interests of protecting the constituent members of the elite oligarchy, and not in the interests of advancing the legitimate participation of citizens or, within the university, of academics, students and ancillary supporting staff.

Here is a telling observation by Wilkinson and Pickett on this. They point out that the process of 'denationalization' of major industries, and the privatization ideology that replaced mutuals, building societies, cooperatives and the like with private concerns 'may have made a substantial contribution to the widening income differences' that have scarred the contemporary public sphere. 'It was common practice for CEOs and other senior managers to receive huge salary increases shortly after conversion to profit-making corporations', they write. What they do not add here is that those salary increases continue even after they become profit-losing corporations. They relate this to democracy: 'modern inequality exists because democracy is excluded from the economic sphere', and also, crucially, from the workplace. And they conclude:

> There are few things more corrosive of a properly functioning democracy and of the market than corruption and unbridled greed. Although the international measures of corruption currently available were designed primarily to assess levels of corruption in poorer countries, they strongly suggest that one of the likely costs of greater inequality is increased corruption in government and society more widely.[6]

In line with this, university governance has come to a position where the undermining of some fundamental democratic propositions, such as freedom of speech and academic freedom more generally, have become implicit primary purposes, and this is related to wider political and social freedoms that are also under strain. Although I will discuss in detail some national governments and their policies, it is in this chapter that the government of the world itself – worldliness, as I described it in Chapter 1 – is at issue, and the role of university in relation to that environmental or planetary ecology.

There is a war on indeed for the future of the university. That war has been preconditioned by national governments and national political economies.

4.2 THE NEW OLIGARCHY

David Runciman explores the current state of democracy in general, and states that, in particular, 'British democracy is going through its worst crisis of

---

[6] Richard Wilkinson and Kate Pickett, *The Spirit Level* (revised edn; Penguin, 2010), 250–251; 295.

confidence in decades'. While pointing out that the underlying reasons for this are primarily economic, he draws attention also to a major contributing factor, in a malaise that is 'institutional'. Many established institutions have been rocked by scandals in recent times: the banking sector in which fraudulent practice appears to have been not only tolerated but almost accepted as normative (and continuing even six or seven years after the 2008 scandals were exposed); the United Kingdom's Westminster parliament with scandals relating to MPs' expenses, which have resulted in various MPs being imprisoned (while, interestingly, some others appear to get off scot-free); the United Kingdom's national press and its involvement in improper phone-hacking and corrupt behaviour in combination with police officers; the police themselves, whose misconducts in many public events of the last decades – from cover-up and systematic slander over Hillsborough through institutional racism, to participation in slandering government ministers and on to misleading public inquiries into criminal corruption – are being revealed at an alarming rate; the BBC, with its history of on-site sexual abuses by the disgraced D.J. Jimmy Savile and others, and – in common with the bankers and other corporates – extravagant pay-offs for failed senior executives; the government's secret services in both the United Kingdom and the United States, whose illicit activities have been revealed by Edward Snowden.

Runciman's analysis of this is made in terms of how institutions have come to function in recent decades. He writes that 'What these institutional failings have in common is that they arose from a growing sense of impunity among small networks of elites. As British society has become more unequal it has created pockets of privilege whose inhabitants are tempted to think that the normal rules don't apply to them'. In short, democracy is being replaced by institutionalized oligarchy.

From the political centre-Right, a similar argument is also advanced by Simon Jenkins. In a *Guardian* article of 7 February 2014, headed 'Bishops aren't the only ones who close ranks in a scandal', Jenkins moves swiftly from a consideration of how the Catholic Church has tried to deal with sexual abuse of children by its priests to a more general state of institutional affairs. He notes that in the face of such crimes, the Catholic Church appears to have had, as its primary aim, the maintenance of its own institutional authority and power. If the price of this is the cover-up of crimes of the most horrific nature committed against children, then, as I'll put it, 'so be it' (or, in Hebrew, 'Amen'). However, the key part of the argument advanced by Jenkins is that the Catholic Church is far from unique. He states that 'any number of British institutions ... all share a curious lack of concern for how the outside world sees their internal practices and procedures'.

In this sense, the institutions are a law unto themselves: while they have a full internal autonomy, they disregard the effects brought about by the exercise of that autonomy – and, indeed, the key purpose is, again, the maintenance of power among that small 'network of elites'. It follows from this that such institutions, according to Jenkins, 'are peculiar in all being vulnerable to a built-in authoritarianism,' their cadres working 'in a framework of professional obedience'. Describing the professions as contemporary 'aristocracies', Jenkins claims that they all 'hold themselves aloof from public opinion'.[7]

What is of interest here, for the purpose of this argument, is that people writing from opposing ideological or political viewpoints have noted the same thing. There has been a replacement of social responsibility – being answerable to and alert to the needs of a social formation within which an institution operates (worldliness) – by the merest form of weak 'accountability', in which the elites who form the oligarchical centre of institutions answer only to themselves, and to the systems or regulatory practices (bureaucracy) that their institutions deploy to keep them in power.

In the light of this, it might be apposite to recall how, in another and ostensibly entirely different context, Sheila Fitzpatrick explored what she calls 'everyday Stalinism'. Through the 1920s and 1930s in Soviet Russia, she writes: 'The requirements of democratic centralism meant that every Communist was bound to obey unswervingly any decision of the party's highest organs. The old qualification that unswerving obedience was required once a decision had been reached lost its force as the pre-decision stage of public party discussion disappeared.' This was part of the identification of 'the Party with its oligarchical centralized core', and, to ensure one's life and very survival, one had to internalize the 'pre-decisions' of the Party.[8]

That is to say, under 'everyday Stalinism', one had to act 'autonomously' by somehow foretelling what the oligarchy wanted, and then exceeding those unstated desires. The oligarchy itself thereby avoids any responsibility for the autonomous actions of those 'outside': they have, as it were, 'freely' chosen to do what they intuit as Stalin's desires or expectations. The oligarchy – including now the university oligarchy – thus welcomes its apparatchiks, preferring and advancing those colleagues who have fully internalized the brand, who have

---

[7] See David Runciman, 'Notes on a series of scandals', *New Statesman*, 31 January–06 February 2014, 34; Simon Jenkins, The *Guardian*, 7 February 2014, 30. See also Ferdinand Mount, *The New Few* (Simon & Schuster, London, 2012). This last is interesting because Mount was not only a former editor of *The Times Literary Supplement*, but also an adviser to Margaret Thatcher, and his book constitutes a kind of apology for the error that was Thatcherism.

[8] Sheila Fitzpatrick, *Everyday Stalinism* (Oxford University Press, 2000), 19.

essentially 'branded' themselves as faithful adherents. Is this a far-fetched analogy? We can see below, as the argument develops.

How does all of this sit with the much-vaunted culture of 'transparency' – ostensibly the very opposite of such Stalinism – that so dominates considerations of supposedly democratic government and governance? This will be the next part of my investigation and argument here.

4.3 THE CLANDESTINE UNIVERSITY

For a number of years, the university has become rather obsessed with the twin pillars of transparency and information, towards which reverence is routinely taken for granted, and with whose demands compliance is always required. Universities are not alone in this, of course: virtually all aspects of public life now bow in pious worship at the same altar: it affects national governments, NGOs and some international organizations, as well as the governance of institutions. On the face of it, the demand for transparency and information is not only harmless, but positively good: after all, who would want important decisions to be based on a lack of information, and who would want procedures to be covert, operated according to unspoken laws – or, worse, whimsy – and governed by secretive and exclusive cabals?

But these terms – information and transparency – are not as innocent or innocuous as they may seem. When our unquestioning respect for them is demanded as an axiomatic good, they start to assume the power of the obsessional fetish, and the price of fealty exacted is high. Transparency and information require our conformity with orthodoxy and dogma for, in principle, they leave nothing for us to criticize, nothing to which we can mount objection: there are no subtexts to be revealed, no hidden matter to be exposed, no subversive attempt to manipulate us against our wills. We have reached the moment where, as Bob Dylan presciently sang in 1965, nearly a decade before Nixon had to resign over Watergate, 'Even the President of the United States sometimes must have to stand naked.' The cult of transparency and information gives us a neo-Cartesian 'clear and distinct idea' of all things, while remaining ostensibly firmly and totally neutral in relation to all that they reveal or give. This is what, in another context, we might call 'data', even 'big data'.

Yet, if 'data' are raw material, as it were, then what exactly is 'information'? A useful distinction between these two would be to say that 'information' is 'data' that has been inserted into a meaningful sentence. Thus, for example, wetness on my skin when I stand outside might be the raw data constitutive of 'rain'; this becomes information when I make the statement that 'It is raining outside'. The same data, however, also allow for a different information, such as

'My skin is getting wet', or 'how miserable it is to have day after day of rain' and so on. In short, information is data from a specific point of view, and its value and even meaning is transformed depending on the point of view from which it is experienced, described or programmed.

Note that neither of these things yet amount to what we can call 'knowledge', especially since potentially contradictory or inconsistent statements of information can be produced from the same data. 'Knowledge', we might say, is what happens when we try to regulate or to adjudicate among competing claims regarding information: it therefore requires dialogue, discussion, and the possibility of dissent. Axiomatically, it cannot be knowledge until it is shared, by which I mean exposed to critique by others: knowledge is precisely an intellectual commons. There is also the issue of the status of a statement such as 'It is raining' as it may occur in fictions, where its truth content can also become questionable.

The condition in which we hold transparency and information in pious and unquestionable regard, while seemingly neutral, holds serious consequential dangers for the university and its proper priorities of teaching, learning, research and scholarly study. In our unquestioning acceptance of their normativity, we have reached a position where transparency has become our poor substitute for truth or critical inquiry as a foundation of our social, cultural and educational living, and where crude information has supplanted the curiosity-driven demands for critical knowledge that are the primary concern of a serious university and its proper sense of values. In short, truth has been reduced to transparency (or the supposed 'self-evidencing' of information), and knowledge has been replaced by mere information (or a series of statements whose veracity can no longer be questioned because they are, supposedly, self-evident because transparently available). Criticism, based on dialogue and the search for knowledge that can be shared in a collective sense, is made defunct and illegitimate in this kind of scenario.

There are consequences for our institutions that follow from this. The demand for transparency and information is now so axiomatically dominant that the real and serious activity of the university – the search for knowing worldly things grounded in debate and dialogue within a community – is increasingly carried out in a rather less visible, even surrogate fashion. In our present time, in short, there exist at least two universities within each institution: an official and a clandestine university.

The 'official' university is that one which is beloved of and recognized by government and its agencies, including university presidents and VCs or CEOs. This institution describes itself or presents itself – 'self-evidencing' – in terms of mission statements, mission groups, research reports, all the colourful prospectuses and websites, brands, merchandise, YouTube videos, bite-sized MOOCs and assorted branded merchandise.

The Official University prides itself in what Bill Readings effectively revealed as an essentially vacuous 'excellence', precisely the same 'excellence' that is claimed by every institution – of course, for who will officially present themselves as 'mediocre'? The Official University is summed up in numbers and figures, finally settling into a position in the seemingly endlessly multiplying and often mutually contradictory league tables that various agencies will use as a proxy for transparent information about the life of our institutions. This is the university that serves the purposes of our own oligarchy: in the United Kingdom, it is the Russell Group of 24 individuals; in the United States, it is the 'Ivy League'; in Australia, the 'Group of Seven'; China's 'C9 League'; India's 16 IITs (Institutes of Technology) and so on. These are all characterized by their self-description as elite (and endorsed in that self-description by national governments), and, like the institutions described by Runciman and Jenkins, they operate by internal rules that do not pertain to the real world beyond their own parochial and narrowly circumscribed institutional sphere. They are anything but 'worldly', and, in fact, rehearse the fundamentally nostalgic or anachronistic sepia image of the university as detached 'ivory tower', a Brideshead revisited.

Whatever happened to due modesty? When did it become important to note that 'satisfactory' had become 'unsatisfactory'? Can't universities be 'good', or must they adopt positions of unearned braggadocio, each outdoing the other in macho postures of inflated and ever tumescent swellings of 'excellence'? The adjectival trajectory – institutional grade-inflation – has been, well, extraordinary, grossly inflated. We have gone from being satisfied with satisfactory, such that 'satisfactory' now means 'unsatisfactory' and needing improvement. Why? Because the new 'satisfactory' became 'outstanding', itself in turn relegated in the face of 'excellence'. However, once everyone claims excellence, the word itself – meaning excelling beyond the norm – has itself become the new norm; so, in turn, 'excellent' now itself signals 'failure'. What next? Well, the new 'satisfactory' is a combination of two terms: 'world-leading' and 'world-beating'. The latter of these prioritizes competition, in which winner-takes-all and explicitly tries to defeat other players. The former is obviously not serious in any sense at all, given that the 'ivory towers' in the sector now assume no right to 'lead' anything, but prefer to be led by political or ideological demand which, in turn, is itself sometimes led by corporate power, or acting in deep concert with it. As Wilkinson and Pickett put it, 'self-promotion replaces self-deprecation and modesty' (pp. 44–45). The rationale they advance for this is interesting: 'Modesty easily becomes a casualty of inequality: we become outwardly tougher and harder in the face of greater exposure to social evaluation anxieties, but inwardly ... probably more vulnerable, less able to take criticism, less good at personal relationships and less able to recognize our own faults' (Wilkinson and Pickett, p. 45).

The clandestine university, by contrast with all of this, is where most of us do our daily work, and it's usually – let me be modest – pretty good. As academics, we are not routinely thinking 'how can I trounce my neighbouring scholars' in a 'competition' for research funding where the point is that I get my own institution up the league tables; rather, we just want to do the research, and we welcome good work wherever it is done, be it in any Ivy League, a local College or an amateur's garage. In the laboratory or library, when our experiments or readings take us away from a simple rehearsal of what we said we would do in our grant application, we do not follow the official line of doing-what-we-said, we engage, rather, in *research*. As Popper put it – and we should recall this when we are asked to predict the 'impact' of research, if we were able to predict what we will know after the research, then we already know it. Predictions of the impact of research are necessarily unethical misleading statements, at least for anyone actually interested in research itself, as opposed to money. When we enter the seminar room, we do not usually seek to confirm preset quality assurance agency (QAA)-demanded 'aims, objectives and outcomes' for the class: we know that, to do so, we would need to circumscribe the possibilities that the seminar offers for imaginative exploration of our topic, that is, for *learning*. Anyone who predicts 'outcomes' cannot, ethically, be a teacher at all.

The latest mantra in the information domain is 'employability', in which institutions are now required to compete to show how their own graduates secure the best-paid jobs to help their own graduates pay off their excessive debts. Does any academic seriously want to ensure that graduates from other institutions than their own do not do well, or that they will be less well-placed socially, economically, or in terms of cultural capital? The official university requires this attitude, at least tacitly but more usually explicitly. Activity that questions such a brutal and unethical stance has had to become less visible, clandestine.

Good work is done in all aspects of our academic activity; but it is now done in a clandestine and unofficial manner, and it is done *despite* the official criteria, going in this way beyond the mediocrities that conformity with official criteria – above all, of transparency and of information – necessarily brings.

When a culture – be it political or institutional – contents itself with transparency and information, as insipidly neutral and impoverished surrogates for truth-seeking and knowledge-making, then we start to lose sight of what the university is actually for, and to lose sight of its proper commitments. We also start to identify the institution as a whole with its own internal managerial oligarchy.

The Official University – the transparent one, replete with information – has not only eviscerated but also threatened with extinction those elements in the institution where the serious work – research and teaching – goes on. That institution, if it is to survive, has had to become clandestine. It exists in the interstices of officialdom and has to remain in such shadowy terrain because the university is in grave danger of being betrayed through a system of governance that concentrates power – and even the very identity of the institution itself – in the hands of internal oligarchical 'small networks of elites' (or Popes, or neo-Stalins), who have themselves in many cases systemically forgotten the substantive reasons for the existence of the university as an agency within the world.

It is also worth situating these developments in the rise of transparency and information a little more historically, for their roots lie somewhere in the early 1980s. That was when the currently prevailing neo-liberal economic agenda was establishing its Chicago-School orthodoxies through the presidency of Ronald Reagan in the United States, the prioritization of the consumer over the citizen in the emerging Eurozone, and the Prime Ministership of Margaret Thatcher. It was then that *US News and World Report* started to produce university rankings, the first being in 1982. Almost overnight, the university was subjected to the Chicago-School economistic mantra that 'Science is measurement': its real existence was reduced to only those things that could be denominated as measured commodities.

A little later, and consequent upon the growth of this neo-liberal agenda, comes the very particular form and characterization of a mass Higher Education system in marketized terms, with consumer-customers instead of students. The neo-liberal ideology can be justified only if everyone participates in its markets, and if all human interrelatedness becomes seen as purely mercantile transaction. The university has to have its 'shop window', with its wares clearly on view and accurately described, and a scientific measurement of standards for the 'products' becomes accepted as a means of driving education into a marketplace.

Everything is now seen as commodity, and anything that is not obviously a commodity is either eradicated or, at best, is officially ignored: it goes underground. We can sell 'bits' of information, exactly as we do branded pens or paperweights, and so, to facilitate this, knowledge – which must be grounded in communal civic dialogue – has to be eradicated from the official life and mission of the university. This mimics our civic and governed life as well: atomized shoppers, our finger-traces and prints being tracked as we punch our computers and abandon civic centres or other real people. The virtuous again succumbs to the virtual, and democracy shrinks to one-person-one-vote-no-matter.

Further, it is in this framework that, in the United Kingdom, we see the emergence of the QAA, and of the massive centralizing and homogenizing power that it has exerted over the activities of UK universities. However, QAA quickly internationalizes itself, of course, for we live in a neo-liberal globalized economy, where, if quality is something to be measured as if it were quantity, then it can, *ipso facto*, be entered into transparent information that allows for international and global comparison and mercantile exchange: abstract number knows no national or political boundaries or differences.

QAA has always been concerned to provide transparent information about all aspects of everyday activity in the university, and especially in its teaching and learning. It makes a fundamental semantic error, however: it confounds a concern for *standards* in the sense of quality with a demand for *standardization* that drives the sector steadily towards homogenization. And homogenization can only be measured by reducing the facts of daily life to comparable factors, or numbers. Thus it is that, in the Official University, a module in 'literary deconstruction', say, is 'equivalent' to a module in 'Molecular Endocrinology', and this equals one in 'World Macroeconomics' and so on: all are 'priced' at 30 credits, say. All have been reduced to exchangeable commodities: the content – that activity that we called 'knowledge' – now has been systemically devalued.

In reality, we know that such vastly different modules simply cannot be compared in *any* meaningful sense; but their credit rating can be compared in terms of a crude calculation that equates 40 hours of deconstruction, say, with 40 hours of macroeconomics. The comparison must always be reduced to the lowest common denominator in this way, and in such an appeal to lowest possible comparators, we can see that QAA-accreditation is responsible for a steady drive towards mediocrity, to driving quality – and specifically the quality of knowledge-activities – steadily down. It quite literally 'degrades' quality, by inflating the priority of quantity, and evacuating all serious content from the actual material and worldly realities of what happens in laboratories, libraries and classrooms. If we, in a classroom situation, conform to our stated aims, objectives, outcomes, we will of necessity be *restricting* intellectual activities and freedoms, and so, good teachers and students routinely do not allow themselves to be governed by the 'official' presentation of what is to go on in class, with all the restrictive and limiting circumscription that that would entail. But we cannot officially say this.

In all of this, pure learning and basic teaching disappear from the official record. QAA-inspired accreditation of everything – accompanied now by transparent information about prices as proxies for value – tries to reduce the activities of teaching and learning to a quantifiable formula, as if we were bankers (the very thought!). However, the road on which the governments of the advanced world economies want us to embark leads inexorably to mediocrity and ('everyday Stalinist') conformity, because teaching is not a commodity-transaction. What QAA calls 'success', actual teachers recognize as 'failure'. If we teach to an agenda in which we show that predicted outcomes are achieved, we are poor teachers, for we are thereby limiting the imaginative possibilities of collaborative acts of imagining – which we should call research or learning. We are circumscribing possibility, and reducing the capacity for autonomy of our students. Teaching, of course, is not even a transaction of commodities; rather, it is a collaborative activity that leads to the expansion of imaginations on all sides. In sum, teaching, too, is research, and, in the clandestine university, we do not have the pious vacuity called 'research-led teaching', but rather, we have teaching-led research. But we cannot officially say that either.

In this state of affairs, we have reached a situation akin to that satirized by Martin Amis in his 1995 novel, *The Information*. There, his two central characters enter a pub, where people play a gaming machine, which they call 'The Knowledge': 'The Knowledge posed questions, offering multiple-choice answers (buttons A, B and C), for modest cash prizes, depending on how far you travelled along learning's trail'.[9] The real trademark name of the machine is 'Wise Money'. This is, entirely beyond satire, our present UK university, as seen from the government, and from its Department for Business, Innovation and Skills. Worldwide, it is known as the 'corporate university', the university that mistakes itself for a 'business' or commercial centre. This is what the Official University is reduced to, and the only thing left for VCs and other sector leaders to do is to promise more and bigger winnings (better employment prospects) – provided the pub's punter's take higher-stakes gambles – or get into greater personal debt as a consequence of transferring the costs of education from the State to the private individual, no longer seen as a citizen.

This is *politically and pedagogically* unacceptable to anyone who has a serious interest in the proper activities of a university.

4.4 CONFESS, DON'T PROFESS

And yet, it remains true that information is indeed extremely powerful. Orwell knew this. He also knew that all totalitarian political regimes and all authoritarian institutional regimes have an interest in taking something called knowledge, and *reducing* it to the level of mere information. This is the real meaning behind Winston Smith's job in *Nineteen Eighty-Four* where he

---

[9] Martin Amis, *The Information* (Flamingo, London, 1995), 240.

'corrects' the historical record of events. Orwell writes: 'But actually, [Winston] thought as he re-adjusted the Ministry of Plenty's figures, it was not even forgery. It was merely the substitution of one piece of nonsense for another. Most of the material that you were dealing with had no connexion with anything in the real world, not even the kind of connexion that is contained in a direct lie'.[10]

It is perhaps for this reason that the United Kingdom can – without irony – boast 20 Mathematics Departments in its 'Top Ten Mathematics Departments'. The worst and most serious aspect of it, however, is that, as far as the Official University is concerned, students are nothing more than fodder for statistics, and academics are nothing much more than grant-capturing operatives. They are both reduced to 'information-production' machines, stamped with numbers. What goes on in the clandestine university – research, teaching, the dialogical and dialectical changing of minds and developments, the serious critical questioning of our worldly conditions – is of no real consequence. That is, until the clandestine starts to get its dissenting voice heard, at which point the resulting dissonance has to be silenced, by force if necessary. Hence we also find the necessity of internal authoritarianism in such a bureaucratic system.

The information in the historical record can be changed, because information is now all we have. No one is to have knowledge anymore, with all that it entails, such as critical thinking, or structural doubt. Information is now the commodity to be traded, bought and sold. You can't buy knowledge, of course, as everyone knows (neo-liberal governments excepted, I suppose); but you can buy information. Thus, the task of any authoritarian government is, first and foremost, to control knowledge by emptying it of content. In parallel, the task of authoritarian governance is to empty the universities of knowledge, and refill it with information or data. Then sell it.

For the replenishment of content in our daily activity, we go to those who operate in the shadows of the Official University: teachers, learners, researchers who are actually getting on with *unquantifiable* activities. Those activities require that we go into a seminar or a laboratory or a library *not knowing* what we will have found out when we leave. As teachers, we can give no information, and, as students, what we learn will actually make the world darker, more mysterious, more demanding of further research and inquiry.

And, as in Orwell's dystopia, the Official University is effectively a fantasy, dressed up in figures that are there to allow political discourse to make claims whose purpose is to establish party governmental power. The alignment of the current system with a form of everyday Stalinism might just start to be appropriate after all.

---

[10] George Orwell, *Nineteen Eighty-Four* (Penguin, London, 2013), 36.

When the UGC was established in 1919, with its block-grant awarding powers, the state established a national interest in the university. That interest is essentially largely removed in the United Kingdom by the 2010 Browne Review, which – thinking it was imitating what it saw as the success of a US system (itself in significant and substantial difficulties because of debts, and of what Andrew McGettigan refers to as 'subprime degrees') – paved the way for the gradual withdrawal of state interest completely and its incremental replacement with privatized for-profit operations. At the same time that the UGC was being formed in 1919, too, Virginia Woolf wrote about 'Modern Fiction'. In that essay, she attacked Wells, Bennett and Galsworthy, the established writers of the day, on the grounds that their novels, while well-written, contained nothing of reality. 'Look within,' she said, and we will see that 'Life is not a series of gig lamps symmetrically arranged; life is a luminous halo... [an] unknown and uncircumscribed spirit'.

The clandestine university is the institution whose task is the governance and maintenance of that spirit. The Official University, with all its well-arranged gig-lamps lighting our transparent and informed world, will kill learning and research stone dead, and it will do this precisely because it aligns what is emerging as authoritarian governance with governments worldwide whose democratic legitimacy and mandate is increasingly in question.

In the light of this, it is worth remaining with Orwell for a moment. In *Nineteen Eighty-Four*, Winston Smith eventually finds himself in Room 101. Leave aside for the moment that purely fortuitous coincidence between this number and the number usually assigned to university modules that are regarded as the basic and opening module for any degree, the 'elementary' aspect of the programme ('English 101'; 'Economics 101' etc.). Consider, instead, what goes on in Room 101 in the novel. Everyone knows about it, and it has a mythic status. The reason for that status is that it contains nothing in particular, but that anyone who finds herself or himself in it will find themselves facing their worst fear. The state, having already a massive surveillance operation involving, Stasi-style, 'citizens' spying on each other, already knows the content of peoples' minds, and knows what constitutes that fear.

The society here, in this text, is one that is conditioned by total transparency, in the sense that everyone's life has become an open book for the state. There is no private realm anymore: even the contents of our own minds are 'apparent' transparently to the state. The individual is now literally 'self-evident', or self-evidencing, betraying itself by revealing itself. This is a completely 'confessional' culture, and in this respect it is entirely akin to our contemporary condition with its litany of self-centred and self-exposing cultures: 'reality' TV, confessional talk-shows, 'misery memoirs', Facebook status updates, Instagrams, the relentless and addictive Tweeting of our opinions or moods immediately and unmediated. John Henry Newman called it 'viewiness', the requirement always and everywhere to have and to express a view, usually 'immediately' or on demand, and therefore a view that is not grounded in knowledge, which takes time and dialogue to be formed. In our time, it is less a Stasi that we might worry about, and more our own security services, like the anonymous NSA or GCHQ.

In *Nineteen Eighty-Four*, it is not so much that specific thoughts are regarded as 'thought-crime'; rather, it is the case that any independent or 'private' thinking is itself, axiomatically, a crime: anything not immediately revealed, anything that remains private, is automatically suspect. Confession and self-betrayal are the norm. As in another dystopian novel, *Brave New World*, self-consciousness and the ability to reflect on one's situation critically, has been systematically driven out. In short, we have a situation in *Nineteen Eighty-Four* where transparency has become precisely our poor substitute for truth. In fact, further than this, truth itself, while having its own government ministry, is now utterly occluded under lies, and the lies are justified by a principle of total transparency, by a 'transparent society'.

The parallels with our own contemporary situation are clear. Surveillance by the state has led to a position where it is more and more difficult to preserve any aspect of one's life as 'private'. Privacy has become, for many, a dirty word. In the United Kingdom's Leveson Inquiry into the conduct of the national press and media, one of the journalists expressed the view succinctly when asked directly about an individual's right to privacy, as against his intrusive 'investigative' reporting. Paul McMullan, a former *News of the World* reporter, declared 'Privacy is for paedos'.[11] Wolfgang Sofsky has done a more serious analysis of contemporary culture in his study, *Privacy*, where he outlines how difficult it is, in contemporary societies, to find any private space or to have any communication that is not being watched or recorded. The revelations of Edward Snowden regarding state surveillance of all forms of communication – quite possibly including the one that I am writing right now – has alerted us to the fact that we are all 'under suspicion'. The citizen, as I indicated in Chapter 3, exists no more: rather, all we have are 'suspects', and we are all, literally in a surveillance society, under suspicion. Etymologically, this condition is rooted in our being '*sub specere*', 'under inspection' or simply 'being watched'. It is a bit like continuous assessment, or the 'monitoring' – of ourselves and also of our students – that is now compulsory in the university sector.

---

[11] See http://www.theguardian.com/media/2011/nov/29/paul-mcmullan-leveson-inquiry-phone-hacking.

Further, the relentless invasion of privacy has come to the point where we are expected to become as transparent – and thus as materially invisible – as possible, and the way we achieve this is through absolute conformity with whatever the power structures of our society determine as normal and normative. A kind of cultural anorexia happens, as we become so insubstantially transparent as to become invisible, to be indistinguishable from a normative homogeneous background. The historical subject loses her or his agency and becomes 'flattened' against the general cultural and social backdrop, as if flush with it and not standing out from it. As a consequence, sceptical thinking – which, of course, is a tautology, for thinking is conditioned precisely by doubt and by scepticism, by standing out against normative and routinized cliché – is being systematically denied, for it is a place where one exposes oneself to suspicion. However, is not the university a place precisely for the exercise of thought? It is this fact that makes Room 101 – and Module 101 – important for our present purposes.

4.5 TAKING YOUR VOICE AWAY FROM YOU

In *Nineteen Eighty-Four*, Winston Smith finds his own particular terror in Room 101. O'Brien puts a mask on Winston's face, and, at the front of the mask, trapped in a capsule, is a rat. The rat has only one route of escape: it has to gnaw its way through to Winston's face. At this point, Winston cracks: 'Do it to Julia!' he screams, in an act of fundamental betrayal of the woman with whom he had hoped to find a private space, characterized by the supposed intimacy of sex. In the end, it is through the internalization of a fear and a violence that Winston succumbs to conformist behaviour. The only freedom of speech he has left is the freedom to use his voice to inform on someone else.

Rats are important for the story, and also for my argument here, at least metaphorically. As I indicated in Chapter 3, Jimmy Reid in his great Rectorial Address to the University of Glasgow spoke against what he called the rat race, against the crippling effects of the logic of social competitiveness: 'The rat race is for rats', as he succinctly put it. Coincidentally, at roughly this same time in the 1970s, rats – real rats, not metaphorical figures – became important for the UK government, and they were at the centre of a dispute between citizens and the militarizing state.

Alwyn W. Turner documents this in his history of Britain in the 1970s, *Crisis? What Crisis?* There, he details the effects of a series of strikes by refuse collectors between about 1970 and 1975. As rubbish piled up in cities, uncollected, it attracted rats in their thousands. Turner writes of this as an environmental and civic issue: 'This reminder of the struggle for coexistence between humanity and its oldest urban enemy, the rat, was guaranteed to send a shiver through society'.[12] The terms in which he describes this are important: this is indeed a war, an ecological struggle, and it is a struggle over urban space, over the maintenance of civilized behaviour. Turner goes on, however, to note the immediate political effect of this. This struggle, he goes on, 'was also the main reason for the government taking the unusual step of using soldiers to deal with the effects of a strike, when the Army was sent into Tower Hamlets to clear the rubbish that had become a health hazard' (Turner, 43), and he goes on to note how this militarization of the everyday becomes a repeated response to political action, as in Glasgow in 1975 when a similar strike took place and was dealt with in similar fashion.

Turner traces the surprising and extraordinary prevalence of the rat in 1970s popular culture (including films, novels, TV drama and popular music) and concludes that: 'The recurrence of the rat in the mid-1970s thus came to represent two aspects of the crisis of modern society: on the one hand the disaster of social planning, and on the other the inability of science to deliver a brave new world' (Turner, 46). This brings together politics (in social planning) and education (in science and its promise). This is also the start of a period in which we can trace the overlaps between what is happening in political government and what is happening internally within universities, or governance.

The trajectory is one where, in both cases, we are going to be required to 'govern our tongues'. The politics of government and the management of governance converge in very intimate fashion at this time, and they find the place of that convergence in a threat to academic freedom and to freedom of speech and of expression.

The cultural medium of theatre plays a key part in this. On 15 July 1985, at the height of the political troubles in the north of Ireland, UK Prime Minister Margaret Thatcher declared a new political dispensation in a speech that she gave before the American Bar Association. Shy of outright censorship of the Irish Republican political party, Sinn Féin, she addressed what she saw as the role of the media in terrorism, dealing thereby with a political issue by referring it instead to the realm of culture. 'We must try,' she said, 'to find ways to starve the terrorist and the hijacker of the oxygen of publicity on which they depend'. Lest this be construed as an attack on freedoms of speech, she immediately added that 'In our societies we do not believe in constraining the media, still less in censorship', which seems decisive – until we reach the next sentence, 'But ought we not to ask the media to agree among themselves a voluntary code of conduct, under which they would not say or show anything which

---

[12] Alwyn Turner, *Crisis? What Crisis?* (Aurum Books, London, 2013), 43.

could assist the terrorists' morale or their cause'. As she moved on to sum up this view, she stated categorically that 'Statements in support of the terrorists' cause will not be made'.

By this point in the speech – and recall that this is a speech made before the American Bar Association, an association which knows fully the First Amendment to the American Constitution designed, among other things, to guarantee freedom of speech and of the press – it looks indeed as if she is not only intending to starve the people whom she identifies as terrorists of 'oxygen', but also that she will, in effect, disallow the mediation of their statements.[13]

A midway was found, and it depended upon theatre. From this point, the actual embodied voices of Sinn Féin members, to give the clearest and most common example, were silenced, but their words were revealed in the voice of others, 'spoken by actors', as the TV and radio media reminded its audiences. This ostensibly bizarre move does, though, have serious repercussions. In disembodying the voice in this way, it translates the speech from being something actually spoken to being something merely acted, and it thus reduces the ontological intensity of the speech, stripping it of all semiotic aspects while ostensibly retaining the semantic aspects. However, while it appears to retain the semantic content, theatricalization and disembodiment of the voice actually substantially changes the semantic force of a speech.

There is, in this theatricalization, a tacit acknowledgement of the intrinsic strength of a voice – including tone which indicates mood or accent which indicates location – identified with a particular material body and presence. The mediation of the voice of Gerry Adams, say, makes his actual embodied voice disappear and strives to reduce the value of what is said, by making it a 'script', something rehearsed rather than something that comes spontaneously, *sua sponte*, as an authentic argument or point of view. It is a political sophistry that 'protects' freedom of speech – leaves it transparent, if you will; but does so by reducing its authenticity through a straightforward attack upon the physical or embodied presence of the speaker, who becomes a kind of puppet figure rather than a full human participant in debate.

In short, the speaking subject, the speaking 'I', is divorced from the historical agent, the 'I' who does meaningful things in the world. This is the obverse of a class-structure in which we are never allowed to address royal figures as humans, but have instead to address their metonymic 'majesty'. However, while royalty speaks as 'one', in a voice that claims neutrality but asserts power by identifying its speaker with her or his agency, the dissident or critic loses power precisely through this theatrical structure that divorces speaker from agency.

---

[13] See http://www.margaretthatcher.org/document/106096.

The parallel in our university sector is that we are driven to a 'government of the tongue'. That is to say: we can have our academics and students speak, as long as they do so in an approved manner and in an approved voice – even, at times, an approved accent or tone (as anyone from working-class Glasgow teaching English, say, in a middle-class or upper-class English institution knows only too well). As Nick Cohen writes, 'The English establishment has a dictionary of insults for men and women who take on the futile task of making it feel guilty – "chippy", "bolshie", "uppity", "ungrateful"…'.[14]

Spontaneous speech – free speech – is curtailed, and the appropriately named 'model student' becomes one who confirms the authority of a teacher by conforming to what that voice says. Likewise, the model academic is she or he who carries the brand: our speech has to be 'approved' in this conformist fashion. This is tantamount to the establishment, within the university, of a certain kind of fundamentalism; or, at the very least, an establishment of assured certainty regarding truth, or 'validated statement'. Only with the establishment of certainty regarding truth, itself based on the self-evidencing transparency of faith or belief, do we get to a state of affairs that can prescribe what constitutes the true, by proscribing dissident voices.

That First Amendment to the US Constitution also protects 'the right of the people peaceably to assemble, and to petition the Government for a redress of grievance'. One way of understanding this is to say that the Amendment that tries to govern by ensuring freedom of speech and of the press works to the extent that it permits the uttering of a collective voice, and of a collective critical voice, against government.

In literary and cultural terms, this would be quite simply the guarantee of criticism – of dissidence – as a valid and necessary priority. Here is one place where government and governance come directly together. Just as Thatcher's move tries to forestall effective criticism of government policy through her attack on Sinn Féin, so also and increasingly university governance structures try to preclude the possibility of the establishment of a collective voice and of a collective critique or collegium. I have already noted how HR principles work to 'atomize' the individual, precluding as far as is possible the validation of collective discussion and debate. How many actual decisions in the governance of an institution are arrived at now through a process of genuine engaged dialogue or debate? How

---

[14] Nick Cohen, *You Can't Read This Book* (Fourth Estate, London, 2013), 35. In my own case, I could add 'prole', 'not working-class but idle-class', and many other similar attempts to put me in my place. Frequently, when one might be in danger of advancing an argument that counters the weaker argument of one's superior, I'm frequently met with 'I don't like your tone', or 'I consider this conversation to be now closed' (documentary evidence *à l'appui*).

many decisions are, on the other hand, arrived at by a cabal of senior managers and presented 'for information', the message then rehearsed by the apparatchik middle-managers, to be passed on down the hierarchical line of management?

At this point, we might also recall E.P. Thompson's great intervention, in the weekly paper, *New Society*, on 19 February 1970, and titled there 'The Business University'. Considering the possible causes of student unrest at the time, an unrest that had led, as in our own contemporary moment, to occupations, Thompson invites us to consider an 'explanatory hypothesis' which many might 'overlook as being too improbable':

> This is the explanation that dominant elements in the administration of a university had become so intimately enmeshed with the upper reaches of consumer capitalist society that they are actively twisting the purposes and procedures of the university away from those normally accepted in British universities, and thus threatening its integrity as a self-governing academic institution; and that the students, feeling neglected and manipulated in this context, and feeling also – although at first less clearly – that intellectual values are at stake, should be impelled to action.[15]

We are in the realm of Runciman's self-serving elite, Stiglitz's 1%: and, worst of all, we are in a condition where these coalesce in an unholy alliance between the university and the privatized capital that neo-liberal governments propose as socially normative. While this may have been considered 'too improbable' in 1970, it is now, in 2014, only too likely – and presented by a Quisling sector leadership as entirely uncontroversial and therefore in no need of debate or contestation.

In his great essay on 'Tradition and the Individual Talent', T.S. Eliot famously argued that 'criticism is as inevitable as breathing' – and, for such breathing of course, we need the oxygen of publicity. In what follows, I want to explore a literary case in which a subtle censorship is practised, and to use that example to show what is at stake in the relations between government, governance and freedom of speech.

4.6 CENSORSHIP OR 'MY LANGUAGE!'

The example is Shakespeare's *Henry IV, Part One*. At the core of this play – though not previously noted or commented upon – is the relation between

---

[15] See: http://senatehouseoccupation.wordpress.com/documents/the-business-university-new-statesman-article-by-ep-thompson/. See also the reissued edition of E.P. Thompson, ed., *Warwick University Limited* (Spokesman Books, Nottingham, 2014), which is worth reading in full. It turns out to have been uncannily prescient: many of the issues that were found to be troubling in 1970 have become accepted part of 'best practice' in many institutions.

government and the governing of the tongue. In ways that I intend to demonstrate, it is a text that addresses 'the intellectual commons', or, differently put, the idea of the common good. It does so through a structure of theatre and metatheatre, which has the effect of disembodying voices and of calling into question the ownership of linguistic authority. Who, in short, has the right to speak, and what governs this right? The play, I will argue, is a tacit critique of a certain fundamentalism, precisely the fundamentalism that tacitly shapes the governance of the contemporary university.

At what might look like a relatively minor moment in *Henry IV: Part One* (2:4; ll.168), Falstaff utters a Latin phrase: 'Ecce signum!'. I want to take this as a phrase that raises issues for us, related to the way in which Shakespeare plays with theatricality in this, and in other plays. When Falstaff says it, he brandishes his sword, as evidence of the terrific fight in which he claims, falsely, to have been involved:

> I am a rogue, if I were not at half-sword with a dozen of them two hours together. I have 'scaped by miracle. I am eight times thrust through the doublet, four through the hose; my buckler cut through and through; my sword hacked like a hand-saw—*ecce signum*! I never dealt better since I was a man: all would not do. A plague of all cowards! Let them speak: if they speak more or less than truth, they are villains and the sons of darkness.

The sign that he brandishes, however, is of course a false sign. It is brandished as 'evidence'; but, while giving supposedly self-evidencing transparent information, it actually attempts to mislead: the evidence is both true (the sword is 'hacked') and false at once (it is not hacked through fighting). We are back in the realm of an 'official' discourse and a 'clandestine' reality.

Structurally, the play operates in a way that is designed to cast doubt consistently on the relation between things-as-they-are and the signs of those things. It is rife with metatheatrical devices, with plays-within-plays, scenes of play-acting or role-play, questioning of orders of the real, as between Hal and Falstaff in Mistress Quickly's tavern, and the world of political rebellion in which Hal will eventually shake off his 'stage-name' to become 'Prince Henry' and, in due course, Henry V. At the core of this aesthetic device is a fundamental scepticism regarding what constitutes the right relation between things and signs: is the reality of the world all it seems, self-evidently through its signs, to be? Can we ever say 'Ecce signum', and, with the flourishing of that phrase, arrest doubt, dialogue and debate?

The action of the play is itself 'framed off' or bracketed off from an external world. It opens with King Henry IV preparing to go on a crusade, in reparation for the murder of Richard II. Yet, within the first 50 lines, this adventure is dropped, to allow for what looks like the historical parenthesis in which he will have to deal with rebellion at home: 'It seems then that the tidings of this broil/ Brake off our business for the Holy Land' (1:1: 47–8). This gesture effectively sets the entire remaining action of the play within the larger historical frame of the crusade. In some ways, the entry to the play matches our own entry into the theatre or playhouse itself: it is a realm bracketed off from our historical being and one where we accept that there are different ontological orders of the real.

In an early play, such as *Love's Labours Lost*, Shakespeare more or less explicitly uses this same kind of structure as something that will become more or less a normative regular theatrical device. Especially in the comedies, but also elsewhere, Shakespeare has his characters leave what seems to be the 'real world', and delve instead into what Northrop Frye called 'the green world' of nature (a forest, an island, a realm of fairies and spirits), before returning to reality and history somehow coming to know the truth of things through their engagements in that purgatorial underworld. In *Love's Labours Lost*, however, we also see the explicit relevance for the present argument: there, the three central male characters agree to suspend their lives for a period of three years, during which they will study. They are, as it were, precursors of those students from Wittenberg whom we will meet in *Hamlet*, and they are precursors of today's students too.

In this kind of metatheatrical structure, we have something akin to the degree as it is currently represented: a temporary withdrawal from historical progress, in order to take time in a different order of thinking. At stake is what we call learning and research, and in these, the key to what we do is to realize that things are not what they seem. 'Seems, Madam?' asks Hamlet, 'Nay it is. I know not "seems" ', and, in this, he encapsulates the linguistic problem at the core of our concern. 'To be, or not to be' is indeed the question; but it is conditioned here by what 'seems' to be the case, by the validity or otherwise of linguistic signs. The theatre, like the university degree, is there to provoke sceptical questioning (the clandestine) of all that appears to be clear and distinct ideas, self-evident truths (the official). This, we might think, is all the more pressing in a text where the historical world is one governed by a religious demand for a crusade to the Holy Land, as in *Henry IV: Part One*.

In this play, there is a much-noted linguistic pun, a site of uncertain meaning. Though much noted, it is however not much discussed. It comes in Falstaff's speech in Act 1, scene 2. The scene is jocular, with much wordplay going on throughout. At one point, though, the wordplay focuses specifically on debt and on paying one's dues. Hal says that he does pay his dues, and whenever that may have fallen short, he has always used his credit. Falstaff's reply is: 'Yea, and so used it that were it not here apparent that thou art heir apparent' before interrupting himself and diverting the conversation elsewhere.

'Here apparent'; 'heir apparent': what is the relation of these things beyond their punning semiotic similarity? The pun occurs a further three times in the play. In 2;2 Falstaff tells Hal to 'Hang thyself in thine own heir-apparent garters'. In 2;4, confronted with his bluffing, he tells Hal and everyone present that 'By the Lord, I knew ye as well as he that made ye. Why, hear you, my masters. Was it for me to kill the heir apparent?' Finally, in 2;4, noting that Hal is mortally exposed to danger, he asks: 'Thou being heir apparent ... Art thou not horribly afraid?'

The heir-apparent/here-apparent issue raises explicitly the question of what is 'here' or what is 'apparent' on one hand, and what is entitled through inheritance of the 'heir' on the other.

These scenes, though, are there precisely to raise the issue – through the device of the gulling metatheatrical play-within-the-play – of the relation between what is true and what is evident, what is 'here apparent'. Yet what is 'apparent' need not be 'true' – as Hamlet well knows, of course, when he asks questions about the 'reality' of the ghost in that play. The play on 'heir' apparent, though, also raises the issue of entitlement, of being titled as king, and whether there is, indeed, any 'truth' or any self-evidencing legitimacy in such claims. And that, of course, is precisely what has caused the rebellion in the first place: is there an authentic kingship? Who is entitled to the crown of England? Who, indeed, is the 'heir', and, moreover, is that 'heir' governed by issues related to the crusades – in short, as King James will ask when he arrives from Scotland just two years later, in *Basilikon Doron*, is there such a thing as a 'divine right of kings'?

Who has the legitimate authority to 'entitlement', and who can claim such authority as being 'self-evident' or uncontestable truth? The answer lies in a claim to a specific fundamentalism, grounded in a faith in God and a claim to entitlement deriving from that supposed transcendent power. This is why the original frame of the crusade is so important in the text. The crusade is precisely about diverging claims upon fundamentalism and therefore upon the self-evidencing of truth.

What does the crusade signify in this play, then? It is, for Henry, a kind of act of contrition or appeasement; but it is fundamentally tied to a religious fundamentalism. Such fundamentalism, of course, has absolutely no difficulty in finding the relation between truth and reality, or between things as they are (ontology) and things as they appear (phenomenology). In short, fundamentalism claims a privileged access to truth, and to an ability to translate evidence into truth: *Ecce signum* is what it says: behold the evidence, behold how this sign-of-things is indeed the thing-in-itself.

Part of the point of this play, however, is to call into question such fundamentalism. As we know, within various kinds of fundamentalism, from Puritanism through to the Taliban, there is no room for theatre. Fundamentalism requires censorship: it requires that the 'here apparent' is taken as self-evidently true. The logic of transparency is, itself, a form of fundamentalism, and it is one, crucially for my argument, that censors thinking. Most especially, it censors thinking about 'entitlement' and about the authority or right to speak or to signify, especially if these are claimed as matters of natural force or inheritance. Theatre exists partly to counter such absolutist claims, to keep a society open, and open to the thing that is basic to theatre: drama, conflict and dialogue.

Framing the whole, though, is another fundamental question put to us by Falstaff. Confronted with evidence that seems to counter his lies about his own heroics against the robbers, Falstaff asks, 2:4: 'What, art though mad? Art though mad? Is not the truth the truth?'

The repetition and tautology here is basic to our contemporary institutional position. It is one where the university is increasingly required to reveal, as self-evident, the 'truth' of specific ideologies, and to see those ideologies as those guaranteed by its intrinsic 'kingship', or presidential vice chancellorial power. In a crude parallel with what Catholics used to believe about their church, their university – like the Catholic Church – is indeed a democracy: one person, one vote – and the Papal VC has it. In the university, the authorized voice is that of the VC, whose HR function is to preside over the brand. To question that self-evident truth locates you in the realm of madness – or, potentially, unemployment – because you are questioning the norm, the self-evident, the fundamental authority that believes that it needs no self-justification. This is the logic of those elites identified by Runciman: self-appointed arbiters of truth who believe that the normal rules do not apply to them, and who can act with impunity. Another word for one who takes this view of their standing is 'sovereign': the sovereign is above the law precisely because she or he constitutes that law. Our institutions are now increasingly governed by a divine-right fundamentalist ideology; or, in short, lacking authority, they become internally authoritarian.

4.7 WHO SPEAKS? WHO RULES?

This explains why governance – like government – has little room for anything other than instrumental activity that conforms to a designated 'line', the line that Malcolm Tucker requires Simon Foster to walk, or the branded official line that academics are increasingly expected to toe. Further, walking this line is, as in the business cliché, also 'talking' it, and our talk itself increasingly has to conform to official lines, above all the line that the university and its work is there primarily to contribute to a specific idea of the economy, as advanced by government. Thus it is that governance and government both require the governing of the tongue.

The turn to Shakespeare, though, is basic to one further crucial aspect of this argument: the relation of the self-evidencing truth to the inheritance of a right to rule. It is interesting that, in recent discussions of secondary-level education in the United Kingdom and elsewhere, there has been a resurgence of eugenics and of 'bell-curve' theories regarding allegedly inherent and inherited intelligence. This, too, has its roots for the contemporary predicament, in recent ideologies. In 1974, Margaret Thatcher's political guru, Keith Joseph – who would become Secretary of State for Education in her administration – made a speech that revealed a mode of thinking that people found rather unpalatable.

The Conservatives had just lost a massive number of votes in the general election of October 1974. Their party leader, Ted Heath, was under pressure, and Keith Joseph was at the time viewed as a possible alternative leader. However, in his first major statement after the failure in the election, he spoke of welfare. This is classic Conservative territory, revisited in recent times by Iain Duncan Smith, and the 'concern' always expressed has to do with what Conservatives see as the spiral of poorer people downwards into successive generations that become dependent on social benefits. Keith Joseph spoke of a 'high and rising population' of children who were 'born to mothers least fitted to bring children into the world and to bring them up … Some are of low intelligence, most of low educational attainment', and he concluded that 'the balance of our population, our human stock, is threatened'.[16]

Despite his own Jewish origins, it appeared not to have occurred to him that such statements were reminiscent of Nazism, and of earlier 20th-century interests in eugenics. Yet the speech reveals what has been a recurring pattern in recent decades, regarding the divergent 'rights' of people to speak, the huge divisions in authority or in the legitimacy of the *vox populi*. This is replicated in education, where all the research demonstrates conclusively that the 'privileges' of a higher education pass from generation to generation of the richer constituencies of society. It is for this reason that governments – and our structures of governance – have had to stress widening participation as a key aspect of policy.

It might be better, however, if we faced up instead to the fundamental issues behind such thinking and such politics in the first place.

---

[16] As quoted in Turner, *Crisis?* (Aurum Press, London) 119.

Who speaks, and who inherits the language in ways that allow for the speaking subject to be aligned with the agent of history? Who, in short, has a legitimate right to the freedom to speak, and how does that sit with inherited rights, or rights claimed purely as a result of inheritance? Who, in brief, has inherited the language in which any free speech might be spoken?

Inherited right is, as it were, a specific kind of fundamentalism, grounded in a geneticism that is supposedly 'self-evident': physiognomically, 'rights' are written on the surface of the body, and likewise, non-rights can be tattooed there too, like the branding of an animal that designates ownership. The problem with fundamentalism is, of course, that God or whatever the transcendental fundamental entity or ground of our truth is called, is not here apparent, and so, the best that can be done is to claim access – falsely and in authoritarian fashion – to fundamental truth. *Henry IV: Part One*, though, is really about the falsity of any such fundamentalism, and especially about the fundamentalism involved in what will become formulated as a divine right of kings, a right claimed to be from God that gives the king an ultimate claim upon right, upon truth, and upon the identity of people. Where does sovereignty lie, and whom does it need to censor, whose tongues does it need to de-legitimize, in order to assert its authority?

Theatre – and, in the Shakespeare example that I have examined, metatheatre – is about reclaiming some basic political rights: freedom of speech in a common pursuit of knowledge, set against a hierarchical authoritarianism of unearned power. In short, in our contemporary marriage of government and governance, there is no room for that revolutionary form of theatre that Schiller, in his *Letters on Aesthetic Education*, designated as *Spielen*, play. If everything must be counted and accounted for – including how one spends each minute of the day – then the very idea of there being room for 'play' is effectively dismissed. Play, in this sense, is at odds with 'efficiency', and especially with the alleged efficiency of human resources in a line-managed system.

It is at odds with efficiency precisely because it entertains doubt, and because it suggests that, as in something called proper research or learning, we must 'try things out', see how they play out. Play, in a different sense, also connotes a certain 'looseness', an uncertainty, a lack of fixity, as when we talk of the play in a hinge, say, where a door does not quite fit its proper space. Play is at odds precisely with such 'property' and such 'propriety' or fitness. Yet it is crucial to research and to learning. One might be tempted to think that this is why it is regarded as suspect both politically in government (where children are systematically denied opportunity for open play) and governance (where students, but above all academic staff, are systematically denied the possibility of not being sure, not knowing, genuinely 'essaying' things). We have revived Gradgrind, and brought him into the university and school.

In some of the world's advanced democracies, we see the odd coincidence between democracy and inherited rule, be it from Gandhi to Gandhi, from George H. Bush to George W. Bush, the 'Kennedy clan', the Rockefellers, Pierre and Justin Trudeau, and so on – not to mention the more obvious case of the non-democratic Kim dynasty in North Korea, for examples. In some places, where democracy sits alongside monarchy, we get constitutional arrangements whereby the monarchy is inherited, but rule and power are contested. It is this latter that is of interest.

It returns us to the state of affairs where we began in this final chapter, with David Runciman. Essentially, what we see now is a view of democracy as something whereby power is contested, certainly; but contested only among those elites who have the right to speak or the right to be heard. And *quis custodiet*? Who decides who has this right? In these societies there are, as it were, official voices and clandestine voices, and it is the official voices that arrogate to themselves this right. Censoriousness and censorship both follow, and so, critical or dissident voices, even voices with the wrong tone or accent – and with them, the whole processes of research, teaching, knowledge in an open and liberating collegium – have to go underground, clandestine.

In the university sector, it is primarily those who speak in concert with those official political voices who get the right, and the speech of others is belittled or demeaned. This is what we call 'managerialism', which gives absolute priority to those who are the institution's so-called 'management' (not even managers, for that would identify them too much as individuals). It depends on a system whereby nobody 'in charge' actually manages anything, and thereby nobody in charge can be held responsible for anything: instead of human beings engaging and making managed choices, managerialism constructs bureaucratic systems that determine what is to be done in any given case. Procedures and processes replace the content of management. Moreover, those procedures increasingly serve the function of guaranteeing the validity of the processes and procedures themselves: and managerialism is management reduced to the observance of protocols. If it can be shown in any given case that protocol has been followed, then decisions following from that observance of protocol are given credence and viability. The result is that we have decisions that may be entirely legal, in that they conform to protocol and procedure; but they lack legitimacy, in that no one actually engages with the thinking required to make – and to give *legitimate* authority to – those decisions.

This brings us close to the end of the present argument. We live, we are always told, in times of rapid change; change, we are told, is endemic. We might therefore ask why nothing ever changes, and why it always remains the same. Why is it that progress towards democratic participation in societies that seek to enhance freedom and to extend justice is seemingly stalled?

One answer is that managerialism actually stifles change, while ostensibly promising not just change but also innovation. It stifles change precisely because it reduces all content to form, to procedure and practice. It matters little, we know, what research is done; all that matters is that the research grant has been captured. It matters little what goes on in the classroom, as long as the students complete a survey showing favourable figures for official and audited report. The entire process is carried out, as with government, in order to keep those already in power maintained in power. If they cannot obtain it by inheritance, they will obtain it by the stealth of protecting themselves as elites.

Just as governments increasingly serve the 1%, so also university governance serves the whim or will of the President, VC, CEO and their central team. Do they care about the university? Do they care about free speech? Increasingly, the answer is obvious, clear and quite undoubtedly shocking: No.

Should we care about the university? To do so would necessitate our thinking seriously about the worldliness of our institutions, their commitments to the material and historical world. This entails change, and the university should play its part in bringing about that change. It cannot survive if it is reduced to being the mere handmaiden and servant of the 1%. So, yes, we should care, if we care about the 99%.

And so should we care about the 99%? To do so would necessitate our thinking about citizenship, and its place in the possible emergence of democracy, or what we might call widened participation in the franchise. The state of affairs we must contest is that where the franchise is essentially being withdrawn from serious universal suffrage back to pre-Victorian states of affairs in which the vote was dependent upon ownership of land and wealth or inherited privilege. Joseph Stiglitz rightly worries that democracy has been changed in recent times: no longer 'one person, one vote', but 'one dollar, one vote'. That way lies corruption, and it is at work in many so-called democracies. Against pre-Victorian privilege, where votes depended upon land, we can say instead that 'This land is our land', this world is our world, and the university should care about the constitution of this 'we', this collective and pluralized subject and agent of historical change: the citizens whose being-together constitutes historical realities.

The university in our time sits uneasily between world and citizen, and it is this unease that has to be encouraged. The alternative is what we are currently seeing: the disappearance of the university as an institution, with the corollary disappearance of citizenship, and the eventual transfer of ownership of history, language, meaning and worldliness itself to the 1% who bask in unearned authority. We are in danger of falling into a predicament where that 1% increasingly steal our wealth, via structural financial debt, and, where required, they can use various forms of force to acquire and retain that commonly shared wealth.

Surely the university should have something to say about this?

INDEX

academic freedom 5, 13–14, 19, 24–5, 39, 41, 54–5, 58, 60–1, 107–15, 129ff
Adams, Gerry 130
Agarwal, Anant 65
Amis, Kingsley 9–12, 98
Amis, Martin 124
Arendt, Hannah 20–1, 24–6, 38, 50–1, 54, 70, 114
Aristotle 31
Arnold, Matthew 3
Arthur, Michael 71–2

Badiou, Alain 73
banks 42, 66–7, 80ff, 116, 123–4
Barnett, Ron 40
Barthes, Roland 15–16
Bellow, Saul 13
Benjamin, Walter 52
Bennett, Arnold 126
Bevan, Nye 64
Bhandar, Brenna 89–90
Blair, Tony 108, 111
Bloom, Allan 53
Bloom, Harold 53
Blumenberg, Hans 17
Bourdieu, Pierre 12, 88–9
Bradbury, Malcolm 12–13, 98
Braudel, Ferdinand 36–7
Browne, David 110n3
Browne, John 22, 42–3, 101, 126
Bush, George W. 80
Butler, R.A.B. 10, 12

Cameron, David 45, 79, 111
campus novel 3, 9–14, 98
Cassirer, Ernst 17
Chakraborrty, Aditya 32

Chang, Ha-Joon 84–6
Chaplin, Charlie 112
Cicero 92
Cimino, Michael 15–16
class (see also 'elitism') 5–6, 9–12, 14
Coetzee, J.M. 13
Cohen, Nick 107, 131
Cohn-Bendit, Daniel 26–7, 37
collegium 23, 47, 56–7, 62, 73, 90, 100–1, 104, 113, 139
Collini, Stefan 22–3, 44, 50–1, 76, 113–4
Confucius 58–9
Cook, Robin 111
corruption 19, 31–2, 38–9, 43, 68–70, 79, 92, 108, 115–6, 121, 140
Cowles, Alfred 104

Davies, David 29
Dearing, Ron 110
debt 18, 23, 46ff, 81, 100–1, 121, 124, 126, 134–5, 141
Dee, John 79
Delbanco, Andrew 50–1
democracy 19, 26, 33–5, 37–9, 41, 55, 57–8, 61, 69, 86, 88, 92, 95, 99, 111–18, 122, 126, 136, 139–40
Depp, Johnny 92, 97
Derrida, Jacques 37–8, 73
Dillow, Chris 112
D'Souza, Dinesh 53
Dury, Ian 97
Dylan, Bob 20, 80, 118

Eisenhower, Dwight D. 24–7
Eliade, Mircea 16
Elias, Norbert 103

Eliot, George 46, 48–9, 53
Eliot, T.S. 51, 53, 95, 132
elitism 5–6, 37, 57, 82–3, 88–9, 92–9, 116–17, 120, 130, 135, 139–40
Emerson, Lake and Palmer 97

Farmer, Alan B. 79
Filo, John 27
Fish, Stanley 13
Fisher, Herbert 4
Fitzpatrick, Sheila 117
Forster, E.M. 104–5
freedom 19, 24–5, 33, 51–3, 70, 80, 115ff, 140
Frye, Northrop 134

Galsworthy, John 126
Gaulle, Charles de 39, 114
G.I. Bill 3
Godard, Jean-Luc 37

Haldane, Richard 5, 24
Harvey, David 36, 89
Heath, Edward ('Ted') 96, 137
Hegel, G.W.F. 2
Hirsch, E.D. 53
Hitchens, Christopher 41
Hobbes, Thomas 100
Hoggart, Richard 96
Horace 1–3, 5, 7
HR (human resources) 111–14, 131–2, 136, 138
Humboldt, Alexander von 41

Ianucci, Armando 109
inequality 28, 30, 32–40, 43–5, 52, 61, 72–3, 79, 81, 84, 89, 93–5, 120–1

Jagger, Mick 97
Jaspers, Karl 5, 25
Jefferson, Thomas 49
Jenkins, Roy 108
Jenkins, Simon 116–17, 120
Jones, Owen 96
Joseph, Keith 137
justice 47, 49, 51, 53, 61, 70–1, 87–8, 140

Kennedy, Helena 59
Kermode, Frank 8–9, 14, 17, 82
King, B.B. 47

knowledge 6–7, 76, 102, 104, 118–19, 124–5, 127
Koller, Daphne 69

Lambert, Richard 110
Lennon, John 96–7
Leveson, Brian 127
Levinas, Emmanuel 46
Lincoln, Abraham 85
Linehan, Graham 112
Lloyd George, David 4
Lodge, David 12–13, 48
Lurie, Alison 12

McCarthy, Mary 2–3, 98
McCartney, Paul 96
McConville, Maureen 21–2, 26–7
McGettigan, Andrew 126
McMullan, Paul 127
Major, John 108
management ix, 13–14, 22, 54–5, 58, 59–61, 77, 109–10, 112–13, 117–18, 139–40
Mandelson, Peter 108–09
Marinetti, F.T. 64–5, 69
Marker, Chris 21
markets 31, 33, 38, 52–9, 62, 64, 68–70, 73, 76, 84–8, 100, 104–5, 109–10, 118–20, 122–5
Markiewicz, Constance 3–4
Marks, Henry Stacy 105
Marx, Karl 2, 75, 76
Mazzucato, Mariana 84
Melody, William 42–3
Mill, John Stuart 33–4, 69
Miller, Jeffrey 27
Milton, John 108
Mitterand, François 20, 39, 114
Montaigne, Michel de 75
MOOC 56, 65–7, 69, 102, 120
Morrish, Liz 54–5
Mount, Ferdinand 117n7
Murdoch, Rupert 78
Mussolini, Benito 69
Mussorgsky, Modest 97
myth 5–6, 8–10, 14–18, 48

Nazism 5, 9, 25, 54–5, 103, 137
Newfield, Christopher 13, 56–7
Newman, John Henry 127

Nixon, Richard 27, 118
Nussbaum, Martha 50

Obeid, Maryam 72
Occupy 2, 6, 33, 36, 86, 89ff, 93, 132
Offer, Avner 86–7
Olson, Charles 100
Orwell, George 83, 124–8
Osborne, George 71, 111
Owen, David 108

Piatt, Wendy 95
Pickett, Kate 22, 73–4, 88–9, 115, 120–1
Pink Floyd 97
Plato 12, 47, 73
Popper, Karl 121
Powell, Enoch 108
privatization 13–14, 18–19, 22–3, 32–5, 42–3, 57, 59, 63–4, 67–8, 70–1, 88–90, 99, 115, 132

Readings, Bill 39, 41, 120
Reagan, Ronald 13, 122
Reid, Jimmy 85–6, 90, 93, 97, 103, 128
religion 6–8, 46, 48–50, 79–80, 85
Richards, Keith 92, 97
Rilke, Rainer Maria 48
Robbins, Lionel 4, 11, 98
Rogers, William ('Bill') 108
Roth, Philip 13
Rousseau-Jean-Jacques 99
Runciman, David 115–17, 120, 132, 136, 139
Russell, Bertrand 63
Russo, Richard 12–14

Sampson, George 95
Schiller, Friedrich 138
Seale, Patrick 21–2, 26–7
Sen, Amartya 69
Sennett, Richard 46–9, 77, 93, 99, 101–3
Sex Pistols 97
Shakespeare, William 27, 33–7, 39, 89–90, 132–8
Showalter, Elaine 11–12
Simmel, Georg 38
Sinn Féin 3–4, 129–31
Skidelsky, Edward (see Skidelsky, Robert)
Skidelsky, Robert 22, 24, 31–2, 62–3, 66, 75, 87–8, 107

Smith, Adam 28
Smith, Adrian 90
Smith, Iain Duncan 137
Snow, C.P. 11–12
Snowden, Edward 116, 127
Socrates 58–9
Sofsky, Wolfgang 127
Sollers, Philippe 29, 40
Soros, George 19
Stalin, Joseph 117–18, 122, 124–5
Stiglitz, Joseph 35, 41–3, 63–4, 68, 85, 93, 95, 132, 140
Stockhausen, Karl-Heinz 97
Stravinsky, Igor 97
students 2, 18, 21–3, 26–7, 56–62, 66, 68–9, 71–2, 76–7, 81–3, 85, 89–90, 104–5, 123–5, 127, 131–2, 134, 138, 140
surveillance 23, 26–7, 31, 56, 59, 61, 69, 83–4, 126–7

Taylor, John 49
Tharoor, Shashi 41
Thatcher, Margaret 13, 63, 74, 96, 108, 122, 129–31, 137
Thompson, E.P. 132
Thrun, Sebastian 69
Tocqueville, Alexis de 26
Todorov, Tzvetan 54–5, 61
Trollope, Anthony 44–5
Trotsky, Leon 28
Turner, Alwyn W. 47–8, 128–9

UGC (University Grants Committee) 4, 126
Unger, Roberto Mangabeira 46, 55–6

Valéry, Paul 27–31, 33–4, 36–7, 42, 51–2
Vecchio, Mary-Anne 27
violence 2, 18, 20–45, 89, 100, 103, 114–15, 125, 128

war
    against nature 17–18, 129
    Cold War 24–6
    'culture wars' 13–14
    First World War 3–5, 27–31
    globalization 33
    Great Schism 7–8
    Hobbes 100
    oil 32

war *cont.*
  Second World War 2–3, 9–10, 12, 14, 44, 70
  Vietnam 15–16, 21, 23–4, 27
Waugh, Evelyn 9–11
Weedon, Emma 72
Wells, H.G. 2, 126
Wilkinson, Richard, 22, 73–4, 88–9, 115, 120–1
Willetts, David 70–2
Williams, Shirley 108

Wittgenstein, Ludwig 44
Woolf, Virginia 126
WP ('widening participation') 61, 69, 73, 93–5, 97, 99, 137, 140

Yeats, W.B. 33, 53
Yes 97
Young, Edward 48–50, 53
Young, Neil 27

Žižek, Slavoy 39–40